ANARCHIST ENCOUNTERS

ANARCHIST ENCOUNTERS
Russia in Revolution

EMMA GOLDMAN
ARMANDO BORGHI
GASTON LEVAL
ÁNGEL PESTAÑA NÚÑEZ
VILKENS

Edited by AW Zurbrugg

ANARRES EDITIONS

First published in 2017 by
Anarres Editions, an imprint of
The Merlin Press
Central Books Building
50 Freshwater Road
London
RM8 1RX

www.merlinpress.co.uk

Translations of Armando Borghi, Gaston Leval, Ángel Pestaña Núñez and Vilkens, notes and preface © A. W. Zurbrugg

ISBN. 978-0-85036-734-8

A CIP record of this book is available from the British Library

Printed in the UK by Imprint Digital, Exeter

Contents

Preface		7
Chronology		15
Vilkens:	How Workers Live	19
Vilkens:	On Working Conditions	29
Vilkens:	On Women	35
Vilkens:	The Fiction of Soviet Democracy	41
Vilkens:	Cells in Russia	47
Vilkens:	The Cheka Dictatorship	53
Vilkens:	Rural Life	59
Vilkens:	The Revolution in 1920 – Nine points	65
Ángel Pestaña Núñez:	Encounters	69
Ángel Pestaña Núñez:	Factory Committees in 1920	77
Armando Borghi:	A Meeting with Victor Serge	83
Gaston Leval:	Impressions of Russia	89
Emma Goldman:	The Crushing of the Russian Revolution	101
Notes on Authors		156
Suggestions for further reading		160

PREFACE

Moscow, the First of May 1917. Marcel Body, a soldier attached to the French military mission, is walking towards the Lubyanka Square. He joins a parade with red flags inscribed with 'Long Live Freedom'. Revolutionary anthems – the *Marseillaise*, the *Internationale* and others – are sung with profound emotion.

Body writes: 'I join the participants, I share their emotion, I understand the fierce joy that moves them. That day was my first contact with the great mass of the labouring people of Russia. The Russian people celebrated their much longed-for freedom.'[1]

All sorts of liberals and socialists were glad to see the fall of the Tsar and his regime in February 1917. What emerged in the course of 1917 was not a fully-formed socialist infant but rather a network of struggling communities, seeking to find a way through multiple problems. These were argumentative communities, relishing freedom. Lubyanka Square was then the location for a large Russia Insurance Company – no one dreamt that it would become a synonym for the headquarters of intimidation, imprisonment and execution, for what would become the KGB – Russia's secret police.

A new regime took time to take shape. It emerged after the events of October 1917 and was consolidated in the spring of 1918. Britain, France and the USA blockaded Russian ports. Poland waged an intermittent war in 1919–1920. Socialists and anarchists demanded 'Hands off Russia', and tried to block the supply of war materials to Russia's enemies. Little news emerged from Russia for some time. Inside Russia processes were evolving that destroyed the hopes and dreams of 1917.

Travel to Russia became easier in 1920. Radicals wanted to visit, to see what was happening and to explore this new society. Hostility, solidarity and hope burgeoned: hostility towards leftists who had supported their governments and helped fight a war that had killed millions, solidarity among the various socialists who opposed that war, hope that the Russian revolution might open new possibilities and hope that a new International of Labour might emerge.

The following texts are from five Anarchists writing at that moment: Armando Borghi, Emma Goldman, Gaston Leval, Ángel Pestaña Núñez and Vilkens. They present sketches, anecdotes and views on life in the new Russia.[*] Pestaña painted this first impression of what he encountered:

> through this first direct contact with the reality of the revolution, we began to glimpse the Russian tragedy, without intermediary filters or cloaks. What we noticed most was sadness and seriousness, we saw it on every face. No smiles, not the least joy, not the most imperceptible hint of happiness. Nothing. We saw only sad scowls, profound sadness, impenetrable silence. No laughter, tongues seemed to have lost the power of speech. We saw pain, we wanted to know what had caused it. We had travelled into the unknown; but the unknown always hides its secrets, until knowledge penetrates its sanctuaries.[2]

One can sense some puzzlement. Pestaña did not go to Russia intent on finding fault. He was reluctant to be critical. He wrote: 'How I would have preferred to have been mistaken! How I would have preferred that this could be nothing but the workings of a fevered imagination, driven by the prejudice that might influence me, driven by life under capitalism!'[3]

Many libertarians did not expect instant perfection and were reluctant to express critical opinions. Tom Barker commented: 'Russia is not perfect, but perfectly organized social systems do not fall from heaven.'[4] Emma Goldman wrote:

---

[*] Notes about authors can be found at the end of the book.

The first seven months of my stay in Russia had almost crushed me. I had come with so much enthusiasm, with a passionate desire to throw myself into the work, into the holy defence of the Revolution. What I found completely overwhelmed me.[5]

... it took me more than a year to get my bearings in the tragic situation of Russia. I considered then, and still consider, that the Russian problem is entirely too complex to speak lightly of it. ... So long as I myself was groping in the dark I would not express a definite opinion for publication. But I still would not have spoken to newspaper men even if I could have spoken authoritatively. I found it necessary to remain silent so long as the combined imperialist forces were at the throat of Russia.[6]

Emma Goldman and Angel Pestaña were convinced anarchists, but they were hoping to find a new reality, they were willing to test Bolshevik thinking to see if it was offering something new, or something better.

Vilkens (a pen name for Manuel Fernandez Alvar), went to Russia as a Bolshevik *enthusiast*. The secretary of his union, Marcel Bila, wrote that he was so pro-Bolshevik, before he left, 'that I did not think there was much point in his going. It was the experience of the Russian Revolution which showed him the error of his ways. His evidence is all the more valuable.'[7] Vilkens said he wrote with impartiality and sincerity.[8]

Gaston Leval had reservations, some years later he said:

In Barcelona, I was one of the first to react against that current confusion, and yet, but while being against that confusion, this Russian revolution inspired us. It presented itself as a regime of councils and soviets, it represented popular democracy par excellence; at least it allowed us to have concrete hope, because – do not forget – the Bolsheviks talked of 'dictatorship of the proletariat', and for us the dictatorship of the proletariat meant a revolution in which all the of the people were armed, and could impose themselves on the wealthy owning classes to expropriate them. It was necessary for me to go to Russia to learn that for the Bolsheviks the proletariat did not constitute the people as a whole but only industrial workers, and then that the dictatorship of these industrial workers had to be exerted through the intermediary of the Communist Party, and then that in the Communist Party it was the Central Committee that was in command, then that within the Central Committee it was the Political Bureau which made the law; then that within the Political Bureau it was Lenin who reigned. All that – in the West – we could not have known. Fatally many anarchists and revolutionary syndicalists were mistaken or were deceived.[9]

On another occasion, he said: 'In any case, I should say that when I left for Russia I was ready to collaborate with the Bolsheviks; I did not agree with a dictatorial Marxism, but on the other hand I did not think that things had gone that far.'[10]

Vilkens, Pestaña, Borghi, Leval and Goldman viewed the activities and policies of the Bolshevik Party with a critical eye, but they sought to balance any criticism with a reasoned appraisal of the outside forces that weighed down and limited options. Thus, Pestaña concluded:

> So, as for the Bolsheviks – Russia's rulers, the men who hold power in the name of the working class and of the suffering people – are they alone responsible for these miseries?
> We refuse to hold them responsible for all the evils that afflict the Russian people. In saying so we proceed with the same candour that we used in rejecting and challenging the political procedures and sophistries that the Bolsheviks deployed to seize and remain in power. Yes, they are partly responsible, but for the smallest part, we must add from the off.
> Material responsibility for all the miseries we witnessed in the seventy days we spent in Russia, falls as an affront, a stigma and a terrible accusation against Europe's governments and

bourgeoisie. They are responsible, they are by far the most responsible.

These miseries would have been on a much-reduced scale without the blockade, without the cordon sanitaire, without the guards posted by the Entente† at the gates of countries on Russia's borders; the Russian people would have been able to defend itself much better against these miseries, and [without them things] would not have come to such extremes.

One must absolve the Bolsheviks of this sin. They have enough faults already on their conscience as socialists and as actors in the drama of the dawning of a new world, without also burdening them with ones they did not commit, and sins for which they cannot be held responsible.[11]

These writers had to contend with the reality they found and the criticisms they heard. Many people were prepared to give the Bolsheviks the benefit of the doubt and were ready to collaborate with them. Marcel Body for example became a member of the Russian and French Communist parties.[12] He worked in a diplomatic capacity with Alexandra Kollontai, the only woman in the first Bolshevik government. He survived into the 1980s, working with libertarians, recounting his experiences and translating Russian writers. In 1936, shortly before the beginning of the mass purges that killed millions, Kollontai had a last conversation with him. They found a safe space to talk. She told Body that Stalin would not let any Bolshevik veterans[13] survive:

> [Stalin's] dictatorship brought with it rivers of blood, but blood was already flowing under Lenin, and doubtless much of it was innocent blood. Remember the massacre of the hostages that Zinoviev‡ ordered in Petrograd, to stop the hand

† The allied victors in the First World War: Britain, France, the USA, etc.
‡ Zinoviev remained in Petrograd when the government relocated to Moscow in 1918, He was, in addition to being the primary governor of this northern commune, the chief of the new Communist International (the

of the Socialist-Revolutionary terrorists. How many decades will Russia need before it achieves a regime of freedom? I do not know.[14]

Veteran communists like Kollontai recognised that unlimited power had been concentrated in the hands of Stalin and that neither they nor other members of the Communist Party could control him or curtail his murderous intent. What passed as 'official communism' sought to censor and destroy both persons and critical opinions. It sought to limit and constrain the thinking of the left, to equate all things socialist with all things Stalinist.

Outside Russia the libertarian press facilitated ongoing discussion, carrying reports and letters from exiles and from visitors to Russia, from critical communists and libertarians. It published the views of organisations[15] and writers: Alexander Berkman,[16] Luis Fabbri,[17] Anatol Gorelik,[18] Gregory Maxsimov,[19] Ida Mett,[20] Rudolf Rocker,[21] Voline,[22] and Efim Yartchuk.[23]

The texts below served as paving stones challenging spin and disinformation. If the revolution in Russia is to be remembered as an eruption of liberation these anarchists should be remembered too: they defended freedom, they contested lies, and they began to work out what was worth keeping and what was not.

• • •

Some terms have been updated in these texts: for example, 'Bolsheviks' has been substituted for the word used by Emma Goldman (Bolsheviki), and 'Marxist' has been used rather than Marxian. Square brackets indicate editorial changes introduced in this edition. Footnotes and endnotes have been added by the publisher.

I would like to thank Marianne Enckell and CIRA Lausanne for their help providing the texts of *Le Libertaire*.

AWZ

Comintern, or Third International).

NOTES

1. Marcel Body, *Au cœur de la Révolution*, Paris: Éditions de Paris, 2003, p. 34.
2. Ángel Pestaña Núñez, *Setenta días en Rusia: Lo que yo vi*, Barcelona, Tipografia Cosmos, 1924, p.14. http://www.saber.es/web/biblioteca/libros/setenta-dias-rusia/setenta-dias-rusia.pdf
3. See below, Ángel Pestaña Núñez, *Encounters*.
4. A sailor, working with the FORA and IWW, *Industrial Pioneer*, Vol.1 No. 3, April 1921; https://libcom.org/files/Industrial%20Pioneer%20April%201921.pdf
5. See below, Emma Goldman, *The Crushing of the Russian Revolution*, 'A Visit to Peter Kropotkin'.
6. Introduction to *The Crushing of the Russian Revolution*.
7. *Le Libertaire*, 18 February 1921, quoted in David Berry, *A History of the French Anarchist Movement, 1917–1945*, Westport: Greenwood Press, 2002, p. 87.
8. *Le Libertaire*, 21 January 1921. Augustin Souchy also noted that Vilkens had started off excusing any faults he saw in the Bolshevik regime and saw him at first as a 'dogmatic Marxist'; later he and Vilkens travelled together in the Ukraine and Vilkens changed his opinions – Souchy called him a true, sincere and honest revolutionary. *Le Libertaire*, 25 March 1921.
9. *Anarchici e anarchia nel mondo contemporaneo: Atti del Convegno Torino, 5, 6 e 7 dicembre 1969*, Turin: Fondazione Luigi Einaudi, 1971, pp. 533–34.
10. 'La dernière entrevue avec Gaston Leval', http://gaston-leval-fa.org/texte.php; 1 September 1978. From: Antonio Albiñana, Mercedes Arancibia, 'La última entrevista con Gastón Leval', in *Tiempo de historia*. Year IV, No. 46, (1 September 1978), pp. 10–21.
11. Ángel Pestaña Núñez, *Setenta días en Rusia. Lo que yo vi*, op. cit., p. 212.
12. Body was expelled from the French Communist Party in May 1928.
13. Kollontai was one of a handful of old Bolsheviks allowed to survive. Stalin may have believed that she would not speak out, or pose a danger to him.
14. Marcel Body, *Au cœur de la Révolution*, op. cit., pp. 294–95; 299.
15. A statement from Russian Anarcho-Syndicalists, brought out of Russia by Vilkens, was published in *Le Libertaire* in 7 and 21 January 1921; it called for action to stop arms being delivered to counter-revolutionaries attacking Russia; it looked forward to revolution in other countries, but not like the revolution in Russia: 'Don't let state communism be established in your countries.' Gregory P. Maxsimov, *The Guillotine at Work*, (Two Volumes, first published Chicago: Chicago Section of the Alexander Berkman Fund, 1940.) Volume 2, p. 445; https://libcom.org/library/guillotine-work-part-2-data-documents. See also: Wayne Thorpe, *'The Workers Themselves': revolutionary syndicalism and*

      international labour, 1913–1923, Dordrecht: Kluwer, 1989, p. 177.
16 Alexander Berkman, *The Russian Tragedy*, Sanday, Cienfuegos Press, 1976, (first published 1925).
17 Luis Fabbri, *Dictature et Révolution*, Paris: Monde Libertaire, 1986, (first published 1921–22).
18 Anatol Gorelik, *El anarquismo en la revolución rusa*, Buenos Aires: Libros de Anarres, 2007. (first serialised in *La Antorcha*, 1925).
19 Gregory P. Maxsimov, *The Guillotine at Work, Volume 1*, Sanday, Orkney: Cienfuegos Press, 1979. (First published 1940.) *Volume 2*, https://libcom.org/library/guillotine-work-part-2-data-documents
20 Ida Mett, *The Kronstadt Commune*, London, Solidarity, 1973, (first published 1948).
21 Rudolf Rocker, *Der bankerott des russischen staatskommunismus*, 1921; *Les Soviets trahis par les Bolsheviks*, Paris: Spartacus, 1973.
22 Voline, *The Unknown Revolution*, Detroit & Chicago: Black & Red and Solidarity, 1974, (first published 1946).
23 Efim Yartchuk, *Kronstadt in the Russian Revolution*, London: Kate Sharpley Library, 1996 (first published as *Kronshtadt v russkoi revoliutsii*, 1923).

CHRONOLOGY

1913: International Syndicalist meeting in London.

1914: August: First World War begins; most of the Socialist (second) International supports the war effort; September: London international Anarchist congress cancelled; Italian Syndicalist Union (USI) expels pro-war minority, Borghi becomes USI national secretary.

1915: International anti-war manifesto. Anti-war conference in El Ferrol, with libertarians from Spain, Portugal and Brazil creating an ephemeral International Workers' Association.

1917: **Russia** – February, revolution, fall of the Tsar; October: second revolution, Bolsheviks take power. **Ukraine** – Anarchist and Makhnovist movements organise. **USA** – joins First World War, 'Palmer' raids on IWW offices, repression of radicals and leftists, Emma Goldman imprisoned.

1918: March, Treaty of Brest-Litovsk; November, end of First World War. **Italy** – Borghi released from internment. **Ukraine** – fought over and occupied by Germany and Austria, Nabat organisation formed. **USA** – Mass imprisonment of IWW leaders.

1919: June, Treaty of Versailles. March: Foundation of the Third International. **Argentina** – Bloody or 'Tragic' Week, some 1,300 killed, 55,000 arrests; anarchists arrested, papers and offices closed. **Italy** – March: April: factory occupations, fascists burn offices of *Avanti*. **Russia** – September: Left SRs and some anarchists bomb Moscow Communist Party HQ; other anarchists disavow this action. War with Poland. **Spain** – Mass

'Canadiense' strike in Barcelona, the CNT, some 800,000 strong, holds congress in Madrid, adopts libertarian communism as its goal and affiliates to the Third International. Managers launch a wave of assassinations of libertarian labour (CNT) leaders. **Ukraine** – Makhnovist army defeats Denikin, Nabat congress, Trotsky publishers order #1824, outlawing libertarians. **USA** – Seattle general strike; deportation of radicals and Anarchists, including Emma Goldman.

1920: 19 July–7 August: Second congress of the Third International; followed by (1) discussions on formation of a Red Union International, and (2) informal discussions among Libertarian syndicalists. 16–20 December: Anarchist-Syndicalists hold congress in Berlin. **Argentina** – series of violent confrontations and strikes in Patagonia, 1,500 killed. September, FORA-V congress. **Italy** – April: Turin strikes defeated. June: Soldiers' revolt in Ancona aided by local anarchists, 500 arrests. 14 August: Borghi arrives in St Petersburg for Third International congress. Factory occupations. Mid-September: Borghi arrives back in Italy, he is arrested in October; fascist squads begin to organise. **Russia** – January: Emma Goldman arrives in St Petersburg. August: Red Army defeated near Warsaw. Autumn: Red Armies defeat whites, end of the civil war. November: an Anarchist-Communist congress about to meet in Kharkov is forestalled by mass arrests; Bolsheviks turn on Makhnovist former allies, hundreds executed. **Spain** – 'Ley de fugas' adopted to facilitate murder of prisoners trying to escape; Pestaña travels to Russia (26 June–6 September) to attend Third International congress. Four-month long Rio Tinto strike. 36 CNT leaders imprisoned in Minorca. **Ukraine** – August: Nabat congress, November: Red army turns on and defeats Makhnovist army. **USA** – Sacco and Vanzetti arrested, Palmer raids target the IWW.

1921: 3–19 July: third congress of the Third International; Foundation congress of the 'Red' (Communist) trade union International. **Argentina** – defeat of a port and maritime workers' strike; Chaco strike, workers' massacre. **France** – May: Besnard becomes secretary of the Revolutionary Syndicalist CSR central committee. July: CGT splits, CSR revolutionaries expelled, they go on to form the CGTU; December: CGTU committees led by libertarians. **Italy** – March: bomb explosion in Milan theatre, set off by individualist anarchists. USI and labour centres attacked. July: Borghi and other libertarians released. August: peace pact between fascists and socialists. **Russia** – March: Kronstadt revolt defeated. July: libertarian prisoners go on hunger strike. December: Emma Goldman and Alexander Berkman leave Russia. November 1921– January 1922: Anarchist prisoners (Fedorov, Feldman, Gorelik, Maximov, Michailov, Mratchny, Voline, Vorobiov, Yarchuk, Youdin) and their families forcibly or voluntarily leave Russia. **Spain** – Assassination of government leader Eduardo Dato Iradier by three anarchists. Pestaña imprisoned throughout the year. **USA** – Sacco and Vanzetti condemned to death.

1922: June: syndicalist conference in Berlin; 25 December 1922–2 January 1923: formation in Berlin of the syndicalist International Workers' Association. **France** – CGTU congress in Saint Etienne, libertarian syndicalist revolutionaries in minority, French Communist Party begins to dominate. **Italy** – February: workers' alliance formed (CGL, UIL, USI, dockers, rail-workers). March: USI congress in Rome, Borghi and his allies reject Third International. August: general strike fails. Fascist violence spreads. October: Mussolini appointed Prime Minister. Labour movement pulverised. **Russia** – Stalin becomes CP general secretary. **Spain** – Pestaña publishes report on Russia: *Consideraciones y juicios acerca de la Tercera Internacional* and attends CNT conference (June) which decides to move towards the formation of a new IWA; August: Pestaña escapes assassination but is seriously wounded.

How Workers Live[1]
'Vilkens' (Manuel Fernandez Alvar)

We visited many factories in Moscow, Kharkov, Kiev, Odessa and other industrial regions in Russia. Workers did not tell us that they were happy about being forced to make sacrifices for the proletarian state. Currently, what really matters to them most is their concern to improve working conditions – it is quite logical, after war and revolution, after six years of suffering and privations.

The workers complain – bitterly. They would like to have more freedom to obtain food for themselves, they want greater equality in the matter of food rations. Whatever there is – more or less – should be divided up in proportion to workers' needs.

The living conditions of producers in Russia are not brilliant. Work – such as it is – does not facilitate living. Over and above the deplorable conditions created by war, the blockade and the transport crisis, etc., there is bureaucratic centralism. Workers are mobilised, militarised, forced to work – and if they do not they are punished for desertion or for being undisciplined. Work – for the benefit of the state – is a feudal service.

One has to live, and in Russia there is a terrible fever to live which has given rise to some tragic egoism. People can only think of their own interests; fathers take no interest in their children, wives likewise with their partners, children forget parents – no feeling – and the Russian people are well known to be sensitive and to have loving souls... But the instinct to survive trumps everything. There is robbery, speculation, buying and selling, and killing; that is the only way to survive, and workers suffer most from all these things.

The entire population* of Russia has a right to receive bread from the government. Factory workers get 300 to 350 grams of bread each day. It is black, acidic, and damp, like paste. It takes fifteen days to get used to it, however hungry one may be. And even this inadequate ration is not provided regularly. We visited factories where several days had passed in August and September without bread being supplied. In other factories, the daily ration was only 200 grams.

Workers eat in the factories. They have only thirty or forty minutes for their midday meal. This meal is rather poor, a very bad soup, based on fish heads, followed by a plate of *kacha*,† a type of Russian rice. But each portion of food is very limited and not very appetising. If one is not really used to it one ends up vomiting.

Food is better in the Ukraine. In the great locomotive factories in Kharkov there is a restaurant where one can eat for fifteen roubles; however, it serves three hundred meals and there are over three thousand workers ... In almost all factories there are military kitchens; it is rare to see carrots or potatoes, and the latter are cooked whole, skin and all – on such days *kacha* is not available. Food is served in mess tins, as in the army.

Workers should – in theory – receive in addition, a *payok* (monthly ration), comprising 25 pounds of black flour, 400 grams of butter, eight pounds of salt fish, two pounds of oil, four pounds of potatoes, five pounds of *kacha*, a pound and a half of rough tobacco (*makhorka*), two boxes of matches, two pounds of salt and a quarter of a pound of tea. But all these things are not regularly available. Flour is very rare, oil is almost never available. These products had to be paid for at very low official prices, and lately the government has decided to make them available free, given that the money collected did not pay for the costs of the accounting (which made people abroad believe that money has been abolished in Russia).

---

* Vilkens might have said that it was mainly the *urban* population which received rations.
† A porridge (often made from buckwheat).

Workers also receive a monthly wage, it varies between 3,000 and 12,000 roubles – according to the pay scale. There are 35 pay levels. At first-sight these wages seem quite high, allowing workers to buy a few small things in the free markets. But in reality, they are insignificant, given that a pound of butter costs 1,500 roubles, an apple 500, a box of matches 300 roubles, a cigarette 50 roubles, a pound of black bread 600 roubles, a glass of milk 500 roubles and other things much the same. To survive workers would need a wage of 100,000 to 150,000 roubles each month.

As for directors – installed in the luxurious offices of old [bosses] – they receive sumptuous salaries. They get comfortable homes, cars, theatre, and considerable pay. We met Borissov, an engineer in the management on the railways in Moscow; he received an exceptional‡ salary for himself and his family, he had a magnificent home, vehicles, [access to] special trains; he received some 350,000 roubles a year and various large bonuses. The same obtained for Arkhanov, a general of Tsarist origins, and a railway inspector. In Kharkov, we met a German engineer in the Astoria hotel, he enjoyed a car and material circumstances better than those in his own country. The Ukrainian government has given a Frenchman, Lucien Deslinières,[2] the task of working out a [national] agricultural plan; he too has his own vehicle, luxury accommodation, and all the comforts of the bourgeoisie. The [opera] singer [Feodor Ivanovich] Chaliapin receives 300,000 a night. The prima ballerina in the ballets the Moscow Opera, La Geelser,[3] receives in addition to a splendid *payok*, 200,000 roubles a month. Certain specialists and top persons in industry receive two or three *payoks*, and 50,000 to 100,000 roubles a month.

There are great differentials between engineers, foreign elements, managers, communists, specialist workers and the manual labour force. Specialists are grouped in various categories and receive production bonuses. In the locomotive

‡ Exceptional salaries, above the regular 35 pay levels, were sanctioned by the state for key persons, on a case by case basis.

repair workshops that we visited, workers who produce thirty per cent or more above their assigned quota receive a supplementary *payok* – and so on progressively; a person who achieves 100 per cent excess receives four *payoks*. Conversely *payoks* may be reduced to a third [for under-achievement]. Workers must fetch every provision from Soviet stores, and this entails many hours of waiting.

Workers' *payoks* are just for one person. Women have to work too, and the woman worker receives another ration for herself. Children under sixteen are fed by the government. However, women with more than two children receive a ration and have the right not to work.

Workers are forced to speculate since they cannot survive on what they receive from the government. To make things, they remove raw materials. They make them even during working hours – little things that can be exchanged with peasants to acquire provisions. Workers in metals factories offered us knives, tinder-boxes and other small objects. Each evening, at the end of the summer working day, instead of going home workers go to the villages to acquire food which they hope to resell in the markets for their children. We have seen miserable people travel for twenty or thirty kilometres each evening, and having to begin work again next morning. One has to eat, and as speculation is more productive, workers consider the workshop as nothing but a prison.

Many workers desert, that is to say, they return to the countryside to make a living working. In the factories around Kiev, *there are bonuses for workers who work more than 18 days a month*, but everyone prefers liberty rather than a bonus. When workers can escape work for a few days, they travel some distance, catching trains away from the station, since they have no travel permits. Goods trains then are full of people who travel in this desperate fashion. One current phenomenon: trains slow down a kilometre before arriving at a station, they let workers jump off with their apples, grain, etc. because if they got off at stations they would be arrested and have their goods confiscated – because only big speculators are up to paying off with a bottle of wine commissars responsible for guarding stations.§ It is a common in Russian towns to see a multitude of people carrying sacks of foodstuffs over their shoulders, official or illicit, whatever they can find.

As for shoes and clothing, by law workers should receive a pair of shoes every ten months and a suit once a year. But in practice ... in Briansk, we met workers who asked us bitterly, how could they go into work in the mud with feet wrapped only in cloths? They told us – and they were right – that in all the city one could not find a single bourgeois, bureaucrat or communist who had such footwear. As for buying such things, that was something they could not even consider – even the least suit would cost 100,000 roubles and a pair of shoes 20,000 roubles.

Communism should, above all, be about serving the proletariat, but that is not how things are. The stores confiscated from the bourgeoisie still contain great stocks of textiles; these are given out to clothe communists, officials, officers, etc., the workers are left in rags. Some clothing has already been left to rot, but the masters are afraid that they might have to do without ...

It is the aristocracy of the factory that divides things up, whenever some unusual product arrives [in a quantity] insufficient for all in the workplace. In the chocolate factory in Moscow, certain workers arriving from the Caucasus, carried thirty *puds* [approximately 500 kilos] of dried raisins, but only the communist workers and their friends got to swallow them; others asked in vain of those who brought them: 'Why haven't you brought some for us?'

In the Petchat centre in Moscow we witnessed a distribution of shoes. 400 pairs had arrived and there were 3,700 employees. It was the first distribution in three years, but it was not the most needy who received them.

§ An economic frontier had been created between many of Russia's urban areas and the countryside. The 'frontier' was guarded by uniformed forces charged with seizing food to prevent illegal private trade (speculation) since scare foods commanded higher prices than those set by the state.

Generally, workers in the suburbs live in the same lodgings that they had before the revolution, in unhealthy apartments and often in cellars. We ourselves have delivered letters from prisoners of war in France to their families and met with families in their old addresses. Communists assert that workers do not want to live in the houses of the rich because they are afraid of counter-revolution and its vengeance, and because factories remain in the suburbs and they prefer to live nearby. The truth is that the palaces, hotels and the best houses have been taken over by one of the many government departments, and the rest have been shared out among officials. To obtain a room from the office for accommodation one needs to have friends and recommendations; otherwise nothing can be done. The greater part of the old bourgeois families is still in their own homes, which they share with officials of all sorts.

Workers have more or less regular concerts and shows by second rate artists in their workplaces for their recreation; to go to the theatre is another matter. A third of the seats are reserved for the unions; but there are never enough for all … One day we were at the office of the metal-workers' union in Moscow, tickets for the theatre arrived, and all sorts of officials hurried at once to the person in charge of distributing them, and very soon every seat was taken by a bureaucrat. If by chance a worker does obtain a theatre seat, he would prefer to sell it, this would provide him with some thousands of roubles, with which provisions might be bought.

Employees⁵ live better than workers. Although their rations are inferior in theory, in practice they are always served first. All commissariats have the advantage of provisions for employees supplied by [special] deliveries. Their restaurants are cleaner and their meals larger and of better quality. They work in the best places: the offices of the unions in Moscow are in the very chic hotel *Elite*. There one can find young, elegant girls,

¶ At this time, it was customary in official parlance to differentiate between workers and employees. The former were blue-collar workers-at-the-bench, in factories and workshops; the latter were white-collar secretaries and officials working in offices.

smoking cigarettes, busy powdering their faces, mirror in hand, sometimes typing away, flirting and drinking tea with colleagues of the other sex. They do not suffer from cold, their central heating works. Their heavy work lasts six hours, afterwards they go home: to a luxury hotel. The *Dielovoy Dvor* hotel – we have mentioned its comfort elsewhere – this is where union bureaucrats live, persons who in their entire life have never held a tool.

It is interesting to note the proportions of each class in the population of Moscow. According to a report from the Moscow Soviet Centre, these are:

398,000 children of 16 or under,
250,000 mothers of families,
100,000 organised workers,
233,000 employees of Soviets,
312,000 bourgeois.

So, in a population of 1,293,000 there are only 100,000 producers; there are more than twice as many bureaucrats, three times as many bourgeois, also 200,000 Red [Army] soldiers who constitute the garrison, and 60,000 members of the Cheka.**

Famine, an awareness that work is not rewarded, the flagrant disequilibrium between production and what producers consume; parasitic practices, the certainty that one could not satisfy even the most basic of needs – all these things mean that workers can only end up seeking to get away or get by; workers become indifferent to production, disgusted by work, and lose their revolutionary feelings. Who is at fault in all this? The fault lies with the state. The state is incapable of organising things itself, and yet it shackles by every means the initiative of the masses – even though it is that initiative alone that might remedy the problems of the revolution. Furthermore, we see communists justifying the most lamentable dictatorial methods, invoking mass apathy, a mass apathy that they themselves have created.

** Cheka: the 'Extraordinary Commission' – internal security police force.

Vilkens gave other example of the failings of the Soviet state, for example in relation to the harvest of apples. It took two months to get a good harvest into storage in Moscow. The state took its time to calculate what could and should be done. It then took another month for the officials to decide how to share them out. When they were distributed – three months later – people received 2 kilos of apples, but three quarters of them were rotten. Such things made the state a laughing stock in the city workshops.[4]

There was insufficient fuel for city residents, and plenty of wood in forests, but residents were not allowed to source fuel for themselves. 'The state apparatus did not wish to abdicate its prerogatives and there was a ban on collecting wood of any sort! Wood was waiting to be burnt while the Moscow proletariat died of cold – waiting for the wise dispositions of the bureaucratic masters, who, being quite warm themselves in their offices and apartments, felt no urgency to remedy the fuel crisis.'

Vilkens wrote that the instinct to survive was paramount. 'The proletarian state pretends to organise life and it gives nothing, the people vegetate despite it all and get on with things – although at every turn they have to face law and regulation. This poor people has a capacity to keep life going – despite all the stupid government obstacles; the people all the same are less idiotic than the State, which cannot even manage to provide its black bread regularly and in sufficient manner.' There was, in addition to shortages, corruption – distribution was easier for those who had friends in the right places. Licensed retail and distribution networks employed more and more people – but often had only empty shelves. The official system was not respected even by communists – one could find them too shopping at the illegal and unauthorised non-state markets like the Sukharevskii in Moscow. This state – with all its centralisation – was a failure. 'One might allow that in Russia it may have been necessary to establish a "power" to supplement a lack of social spirit among the masses and to concentrate energy having in mind the struggle against counter-revolution; if this "power" had limited itself to making suggestions, to opening horizons, to drawing attention to errors and mistakes, to giving the masses some orientation but letting them direct themselves ... but one cannot expect such things from a State "power". The proletarian State, like all states monopolises and devours, little by little; it confiscates, for its own exclusive benefit, each and every revolutionary achievement that constitutes the strength, the dynamic expansive force of the regime of Soviets.'[5]

NOTES

1 First published in a French anarchist journal, *Le Libertaire*, 20 May 1921; *L'Antorcha*, 14 October 1921.
2 Author of *Comment se réalisera le socialisme*, http://gallica.bnf.fr/ark:/12148/bpt6k82719f/f11.image.r=Le%20droit%20capitaliste%20du%20travail, published in translation as *The Coming of Socialism*.
3 Yekaterina Geltzer?
4 *Le Libertaire*, 4 March 1921.
5 Ibid., conclusion.

On Working Conditions[1]
'Vilkens' (Manuel Fernandez Alvar)

Given the principle of state supremacy, and the tendency of the state to nationalise and dominate every aspect of economic life, the factory council – as an organ of production freely elected by workers, and continuously communicating with workers – had to be eliminated. If left in their own hands workers and producers might have made factory councils, little by little, into a terrible and invincible weapon. Factory councils had to go because they created an autonomy that was dangerous to the very existence of the proletarian state.

Workers were convinced, at the time of the October revolution, that factories would come into their own hands, that they would have responsibilities, and a direct interest in management and its outcomes, be they good or bad. But they did not have economic organisations ready to manage distribution, and this function passed into the hands of political organisations. The communists rushed in, subordinating factory councils to the trade unions (which were organs of centralisation and compulsion), and, being thoroughgoing politicians, they thought the factory councils would easily be subordinated to their own power. Little by little factory councils were divested of their essential functions by unions, and were relegated to the second tier.

The Bolsheviks, once in power, sought to increase production, but for reasons beyond the control of workers this goal was not achieved as they had wanted. There was a lack of food, a poor pattern of trading for provisions with peasants, a lack of raw materials, poor relations with technicians, etc. The communists said the fault lay with the factory councils; later they said councils were insufficiently energetic, and inept. Consequently, in a meeting of the central committee of the Communist Party it was decided to end [the role of] factory councils as organisers of production. The direction and administration of factories was placed in the hands of individuals. Despite the disastrous moral effects that this decision would have for the mass of workers, who were consigned to being treated as mere operatives in the process of production, the unions accepted this decision pretty much mechanically.

Common sense would suggest that it would have been appropriate to remove the prior causes that impeded normal work, or at least to have tried stimulating the masses, rather than reducing and undermining the capacities of producers in such a brutal fashion. Those prior causes continued and it was an infantile error to introduce military methods to improve production, through subordination, discipline, punishments – thereby replacing one set of problems by another. This turn was in any case both artificial and sudden. Compulsion was applied even among the Bolsheviks – to make them accept it. On 16 November [1920?], in *Pravda*, Rykov[*] bitterly lamented that the current level of production was varying between 4% and 35% of what it had been in 1914. In those industries that were most indispensable the average level of production was 12% of 1914 levels. Moreover, the Bolshevik regime was on the way to shepherding production into [the hands of] private capital – using pretexts that were more or less specious. The Bolsheviks had created the proletariat's indifference, in the process of displacing labour from the management of production, and so had created a situation that was not without peril for the revolution itself.

Factory directors are men nominated by the Supreme Soviet

---

[*] Alexei Rykov chaired the Supreme Council of National Economy, and became Prime Minister in 1924, he was demoted in 1929 and executed in 1938, another victim in Stalin's purges.

of the National Economy – they may be the former manager, an industrialist, a technician or a model worker – cases vary. Directors' responsibilities and powers are – in reality – unlimited. They can justify their every decision citing 'the essential demands of production'. Neither workers, nor factory committees, nor unions can make directors account for their actions. They are the key persons when it comes to hiring and firing workers, they can modify working conditions; to sum up: they can manage and govern as they see fit.

In respect of anything to do with labour, and for any workplace misdemeanour, a director may report workers to the police whenever he thinks it necessary. He is the person who nominates and replaces supervisory staff, it is he who he allocates the pay levels of various [sorts of] workers. There are factories where directors have prisons in which workers may be imprisoned for workplace misdemeanours, for up to three days. We met seven workers from a metal works in Briansk, who for twenty days were locked up every evening at the end of the work because they had gone on strike. Workers on a large building on Tverskaya Street in Moscow were guarded by supervisors while at work, and were then locked in an underground basement, and they had to put up with this until the building was finished. In one textile factory in Tula women came to see their husbands detained after work.

Directors enjoy the same status, have the same authority, and have more power than they had previously under the capitalist regime. When a worker is dismissed, he is given a certificate, which he needs to get a new job; it explains the reason for his dismissal. Within the union of anarchist workers in Moscow I saw a certificate given to a comrade who made clogs, in which the director recommended that this person should not be taken on because he was a dangerous individual, capable only of fermenting revolt.

As for working conditions, these vary from place to place, from industry to industry and from one director to another. Many factories do not work for more than eight hours; in others ten hours or more is the norm; in the Donetsk region, a ten to twelve-hour day is worked. There is a ten-hour day in the Russian-American Tool factory in Moscow, in the factories making locomotives and dynamos, and in the large factory making hardware in Kharkov. Almost all the sugar factories in the Ukraine work more than eight hours, and much the same in every workshop making and repairing military machines and materials. Work begins at eight or nine o'clock, official time runs three hours in front of solar time. Officials and secretaries have only a six-hour day and have half an hour off for lunch.[†]

The Taylor system has been introduced in some factories. Piecework has been re-established in many places; in others, a minimum level of production has been fixed and there are bonuses for exceeding them. All workers are mobilised and militarised, subjected to rigorous discipline, and subjected to summary punishment. Such is the situation that the daily papers, when they discuss work, speak only in a military language: 'work front, labour HQ, work-army, soldiers at work, work-divisions,' etc. Quitting work is termed desertion, and, as such is severely punished. A committee in each city deals with 'labour deserters', it is composed of a delegate from the soviets, one from the unions and one from the Cheka.[‡] Railways, transport and certain larger factories have their own revolutionary tribunals, composed of elements loyal to the communist party, and making judgements in line with their policy. Workers aged sixty are given a medical examination, and if they are declared fit they must continue working; if not they are given a sedentary and less exacting job. To ensure that the Labour Code is complied with there are some four hundred men and women inspectors.

As for the right to strike, the following example is most revealing: it relates to the great locomotive factory in Perovo, on the Kazan railway, near Moscow, which employs 3,000 workers. The workers there had played a great part in the

[†] An eight-hour day had been decreed in November 1917; it was one of the basic demands of labour movements worldwide.
[‡] Cheka: The Extraordinary Commission to Fight Counter-Revolution and Sabotage, the state security police.

ON WORKING CONDITIONS

revolutionary movement of 1905. A general strike broke out last July. The cause was demands about poor provisions and intolerable political conditions – demands vainly addressed to the government. The assembled workers decided to place their demands to the authorities: *the suppression of the privileged ration, freedom of domicile for workers, the right for large families to have supplementary rations, the ending of searches of workers, the right to nominate a committee with responsibility for [supervising] the provisioning of the workplace.*

The Bolshevik power responded that it would study these demands. One month later, no further response having come to light, a general strike was approved unanimously. Three days after the start of the strike several regiments arrived with machine-guns and artillery. Workers were called on to return to work. When no one obeyed, the Cheka proceeded in classic fashion and arrested workers designated as 'agitators'. Intimidated by machine-guns and artillery, the workforce returned to work.

Kommunistisky Truda (a Communist labour journal), reporting these events, said they were a vast plot instigated from Poland, the Poles had sought to provoke a general strike across the entire rail network to prevent the transport of provisions and war materials to the front;§ and that Anarchists and Socialist-Revolutionaries played a large part in provoking it; that sectoral interests should not oppose general interests; that the strikers' demands could not be satisfied instantaneously, etc. ... Four months later, in November, the judgement of the railway's revolutionary tribunal, (composed of Communists) passed the following sentences on the condemned: twenty years' hard labour for one Communist worker; fifteen years hard labour for an Anarchist, a Christian, a Tolstoian, three Socialist-Revolutionaries and four non-party workers; five years for three workers; three years for six persons [... and lighter sentences for some others]. *Kommunistisky Truda* reported on the following

§ There was intermittent fighting in 1919 and especially in the summer of 1920, between Polish and Russian forces; a peace was signed in March 1921.

day: 'This is an example that unconscious proletarians should reflect on.' This is an example, one among several, of how the so-called dictatorship of the proletariat imposes suffering on the real proletariat.

NOTES

1   *Le Libertaire*, 27 May 1921.

On Women[1]
'Vilkens' (Manuel Fernandez Alvar)

Women in Russia must work as well as men. The assumption is that women should find work in keeping with their capabilities, in conditions that would allow them to survive, without being compelled to resort to venal love. Most daughters and partners of [male] workers¶ toil in factories and workshops where they fall under the same regime as men. We met many of them repairing railways, unloading wagons, sweeping snow in towns, sweeping streets, doing all sorts of cleaning, sending supplies to hotels, hospitals and barracks.

Thousands of women – [previously] members of the petty bourgeoisie or of the higher bourgeoisie, as well as women working in luxury trades, have been compelled to look for work. But the division of occupations among women is far from equitable. To obtain a position that is in great demand one must have a recommendation, of lesser or greater influence.

In Russia, as elsewhere, pretty girls pay with their bodies for a place in the offices of a commissariat. There, in the warm, officially for six hours,[2] they have only to shuffle papers, no great strain. Many women make advances on their superiors to keep such an enviable position, or obtain a better one. Commissars big and small, and higher managers of all sorts take advantage of this situation, and choose mistresses among the daughters of the former nobility and bourgeoisie, who sell their favours to obtain these privileged positions.

So, in Russia, one can meet, women elegantly dressed and

¶ The original text has the masculine term.

living in superb accommodation. They can afford to pay 20,000 roubles to have their hair done, and 5,000 to have their nails polished. Cars are at their disposal. In the theatre, they dress in silk, with jewels and diamonds, just as they did in the time of the Tsar. The people, following the current fashion of making names from abbreviations, call such women *Sod-Koms* (mistresses of Commissars); likewise, those who have used the revolution to turn a profit are called *Sov-bourg* (bourgeoisie of the soviets).

In each office or commissariat there are differences between those who have a protector with an official title and those who are forced to sell themselves, because hungry women cannot put up much resistance to the male sensual appetite. Women in Russia are currently considered as instruments of pleasure, to be used according to [the male's] inclination. A woman who has the courage to refuse someone is exposed to reprisals by those who have power over her.

Here are a few facts selected out of thousands. In Moscow, the housing crisis is acute, but X, a Cheka commissar, has accommodated his three mistresses magnificently: one in the Tverskaya, another in Petroskaya and the third in a pretty villa close to the Yaroslavsky station. Officially, all three work in a commissariat

One day, when we were in the labour commissariat, a worker was complaining about having had to wait three hours. The young woman in charge of the matter was very busy reading a novel and smoking a cigarette. Finally, she replied: 'Come back tomorrow at 10.' 'Impossible', was the reply – 'I have to work'. 'Well now I have no time' – and she went back to her reading. The worker, furious, went to complain to the office manager. The latter supported his underling: 'who had urgent matters to deal with!', the young woman was his partner.

In the hotel where we were based, the *Dielvoy Dior*, there were pretty young chamber maids – naturally women of labour stock. We could observe the Chekists who were responsible for security. They often had their way with them, willingly or unwillingly. One of them was the plaything for four of them.

She had to put up with it – a word from one of them would have been enough to have her dismissed.

This August a young woman arrived in the same Petrograd hotel, she was pretty, intelligent and spoke four languages. For ten days, she looked in vain for work. Being without money or accommodation she was forced to act the prostitute for delegates – for her food and lodgings. Having met several, she had occasion to meet Ranizez, the delegate for Mexico. He married her, by Soviet law, and took her back to his own country at Soviet expense.

Foreign delegates were besieged by women from all over, telling them of their privations and miseries, and offering themselves as slaves for life, if only they were taken back to Europe. They would become intimate friends for a meal, a theatre invitation, or a car excursion. Some delegates had as many as six mistresses all at once. The Italian socialists, with B. at their head, were the worst of all. They had no scruples about making promises, and sometimes not delivering these miserable women, or getting them out of Russia.

I was friends with a Red Cross sister serving the medical needs of delegates. One day she showed me a superb velvet coat doubled with magnificent silk, which might have belonged to a grand duchess. She had on her finger a ring with a brilliant gem of superb workmanship. I asked her where it came from. She told me it came from V, a Latvian in charge of the internal security of the Third International, and added, 'I became his mistress for a month.'

A young Armenian woman became ill in the hotel in the room of one comrade. No one took any notice of her whilst she was ill. As soon as she recovered, and because she was a beauty among her people, she at once became the mistress of an influential employee who quickly found her a good position.

One night we spent an evening at the Moscow conservatoire. There were men – young and old – in uniform, or in evening dress, in the room where pupils met. They offered the young women sweets, cakes and all sorts of presents. In a corner, mothers were murmuring along with older men. One young woman said to another, looking at an old gorilla: 'See here, I was with him last night, he gave me 50,000 roubles and a pretty pair of shoes.' The other replied: 'And you know that tobacco merchant made me a very nice offer – but to be honest he disgusts me.' The evening was barely different from any other in a capital city; speculators, high-ranked officers, commissars get priority. The stars of the theatre face the same parade.

In Kharkov, we met a young girl who was eight days away from her family; she was seventeen years old and had had to leave Petrograd**, because she had refused her bureau chief. In Kharkov, she was noticed by one of the most powerful Chekists, and finally, to escape her miseries and troubles, she resigned herself to living with a commissar responsible for army supplies. Wherever we travelled we noticed that Chekists always had girls in their carriages. The girls explained: 'We are forced to lead this life of perpetual travelling, of servitude, serving men who are brutal and often drunk, because otherwise we would be abandoned to something even worse.'

One day, in an isolated railway station, in the middle of the steppe, we met two employees, sent from Moscow to the army in the South. They had been left for three days on the platform of this little station. The Cheka weren't interested. We had to intervene to have a place found for them. At Bryansk railway station we saw soldiers chasing young girls leaving the hospital in Kiev and travelling to Moscow, who had no one to defend them. We knew one trade union secretary who had four typists: they lived all four together with him. One communist, a labour inspector lived in *Dielevoy Dvor* with his two secretaries as mistresses in the same room. The students of the military schools in Kiev and Moscow had hundreds of girls serving, serving them also as mistresses. Thousands of women follow the Red Army for commissars, officers, soldiers and in the auxiliary services. And syphilis, already very widespread in Tsarist times,

---

** St Petersburg.

is terribly corrosive among the Russian people. Radek,[††] a well-known communist had secretaries everywhere. We chatted with a young girl in the *Lux* hotel who did nothing at all by day, and who occupied one of the best rooms. 'I am Radek's secretary', she said proudly. We ourselves, met four of Radek's pretty secretaries.

Other than these women – privileged for a moment by this regime – this system is not fit to attract female sympathy for the revolution. Women who want to be free in more than theory, want first of all to be free *economically* – since this is the foundation of every freedom. We did not see that the current state of things was transitory. This terrible prostitution can cease only with well-being for all, in an egalitarian society and with the disappearance of the Socialist State.

NOTES

1 *Le Libertaire*, 24 June 1921.
2 Applicants seeking papers in government offices queued for hours or days, the official six-hour day was not observed in practice. It was noticed that government offices were warm because there was precious little fuel for the home use.

†† K B Radek, journalist, Bolshevik leader, active in the Communist International.

The Fiction of Soviet Democracy[1]
'Vilkens' (Manuel Fernandez Alvar)

Some selected facts:
Last year, in the large Kharkov factory making locomotives, tanks, vehicles, etc., there were 3,600 workers, but only 58 communists, with responsibility for surveillance, discipline and other similar functions.

Three Anarchists, two Mensheviks and four non-party persons were elected in the Soviet election. The election was annulled. Since the proletariat in the factory manifested its intention to re-elect them, the factory committee expelled them from the factory, on the pretext that they were 'counter-revolutionaries, agents of the bourgeoisie'. They were forced to leave Kharkov some days later. The election was carried through – with only communists participating – and they voted for the list proposed by the Fav-committee [factory committee].

Last September, the sugar workers in Kiev abstained from voting, because no other list was allowed other than that of the Bolsheviks.

The comrades of the *Ispolkom* (the Central Executive Political Committee) of the Rostov soviet, composed of Anarchists, Mensheviks, Maximalists[*] and non-party people – who had suffered all sorts of persecution during Denikin's time[†] – were arrested by the Cheka and send to the Butyrka prison in Moscow, where I met them. Nevertheless, between January 1920 and the end of the year, they were not questioned even once. A

---

[*] The most radical tendency of the Socialist-Revolutionaries.
[†] Anton Denikin was a Tsarist 'white' (fascistic) General whose troops occupied much of the Ukraine in 1919.

new *Ispolkom* composed of communists sent from Moscow was installed instead.

One munitions factory in Moscow elected the anarchist theoretician Gordin‡ in February 1920. The election was invalidated. Gordin was re-elected. The Cheka intervened and arrested Gordin for demagogy, and he was imprisoned for several months. The workers in that factory did not want to elect anyone else, and they were left without representation.

In Samara, the Bolsheviks dissolved the city Soviet because they were in the minority, and replaced it with the former Soviet, elected in 1918, on the pretext that at that time there were more workers there and that they were more [class] conscious then.

Early last year, the grand bakery in Moscow, which employs 1,500 workers, elected a list opposed to the Bolsheviks, but the election was annulled. Afterwards two Cheka commissars, revolver in hand, forced through a vote for a communist list, while the factory gates were guarded by soldiers.

In a sugar factory in Moscow, workers went on strike to protest against the nomination of delegates behind their backs; the factory committee had 3,000 workers sent into the streets on the pretext that there was a lack of raw materials, and the 'delegates' remained on the Soviet.

The list of communists passed before construction workers was composed of a doctor, two journalists, and some metallurgists, because there were no communist [construction workers].

Last December, I was present at an election of delegates from the Petchat centre; it took place in the grounds of an old factory between empty boxes and cases. Among its 2,700 employees, 24 were communists. 64 persons took part in the election, and taking little interest, they let pass a list proposed by the Petchat committee. The following day, in *Kommunisticheskii trud* [a communist labour paper] under the title 'Labour Front', an article was published asserting that the valiant communist cell

---

‡ Abba Gordon was a 'Universalist' (utopian) anarchist; he emigrated to the USA, and subsequently to Israel.

of the Petchet centre 'had held a triumphant meeting and the employees had unanimously elected the communist list'. So, this probably accounts for how communist ideas are advanced, between the proletariat and the centre, with the latter deciding who is the right person to represent the former.

I shall stop listing such cases now; they illustrate the history of 'Soviet' development, and how it is being stifled by the Bolsheviks.

In the early days of the revolution, the proletariat wanted to rid itself of bosses in order to take on *economic power*, the only power that it wanted. It believed in the necessity of electing delegates within its various units. Such persons enjoyed its confidence and were revocable (to prevent any betrayal of its interests). Assemblies and councils met to resolve current problems, and to establish necessary understanding and policies. These delegates, elected in factories and workshops, formed the Councils or Soviets, of factories and communes.

This system, so extolled in the guise of a 'Soviet system', is no new formula. Spanish Anarchists have propagated the idea of adopting Councils for current economic requirements for many years now. The Russian revolution and the Russian people, in principle all-powerful, did not progress without instinctively putting into practice this idea dear to syndicalists and anarchists of all lands; [but] thereafter Marxists, jealous of their own supremacy, did not look on it with favour. All Russian revolutionary parties accept this system, it was something imposed with irresistible force by the people; it was a force before which the Bolsheviks had to prostrate themselves.

One must keep this in mind: that for this regime of Soviets and Councils to be superior to other representative systems, for it to be really an effective and direct expression of popular will, it must be a genuinely be delegated by the producers, it must necessarily be based on pure sources, that is to say there must be; freedom in elections, with mandates that are limited and imperative, and with an uninterrupted right of recall – this is the only way to guarantee the sovereignty of the mass of producers.

Without such things, the system of Soviets will be worth neither more, nor less than the current parliamentary system, or the previous regimes of socialist parties (be they communist or something else) or that of the CGT [French General Labour Confederation].

None of these essential conditions – which might give some value to this system – continues to exist. There is no Republic of Soviets. It is a deceitful system at the base, from elections in factories to those of Peoples' Commissars, who are as much representatives of the producers as ministers are in bourgeois countries.

Of course, Bolshevik literature does not reveal how they messed with popular Soviet system. Soviets have been shattered by the state, and the state is reactionary. The proletarian state is nothing more than the Bolshevik party.[2]

Are workers and peasants freely elected? … For some time now they have been alienated from elections to the Soviets. The Bolsheviks 'manage' elections – just as the French Second Empire did,§ that or even worse – and it is they who are always elected.

We will return to this subject.

Vilkens related his experience in an election meeting for a rural soviet in another article.[3] There were complaints when one Cheka member gave a speech that was excessively long. Insults were traded – critics were called 'Mensheviks' or 'Socialist Revolutionaries'. He saw a person sitting next to him intimidated and forced into silence. Some voters left before the vote was taken. He also noted that Anarcho-syndicalists were arrested when they met for a conference on 24 October 1920.[4] The arrests violated an agreement signed just eight days previously between the Mahknovists and Bela Kun.[5] That agreement had set out that there would be freedom

---

§ The Empire of Napoleon III in which the prefects of each French department were expected to fix results to have pro-government candidates elected.

for anarchists and Makhnovists to promote their political ideas. Makhno's programme included calls for the abolition of parasitism [bureaucracy], for the suppression of commissars, thorough decentralisation, and demanded – as a priority – freedom of propaganda and free elections, in short: 'Long live Free Soviets'.

Vilkens also described how Russia's labour organisations functioned.[6] He noted that membership of unions was compulsory. Of 4½ million members, 2/5 were officials and bureaucrats. The membership of the executive of the labour unions was exclusively communist. There were no local organisations akin to the French bourses du travail (trades' councils). Russian labour exchanges served only to help allocate workers to jobs, they had no broader social functions, and no local autonomy. Effectively, labour had no right to strike. Vilkens cited one example of repercussions when bakers went on strike: their union branch was closed, the members concerned were excluded from election lists for union positions, and their meetings were banned. Vilkens wrote that the French Labour Confederation (CGT) was imperfect – corrupted and somewhat over centralised – but nonetheless there was greater autonomy in local CGT organisation than among labour in Russia.

NOTES

1   Original title: 'The Fiction of the Soviets', 8 April 1921, *Le Libertaire*.
2   Non-communist radicals were already being purged at this time. On occasion members of the Communist Party were also eliminated if they offended some powerful opponent in the party. There were also suspicions that Russian communists would have foreign dissident radicals killed off. Vilkens met with delegates attending the second Comintern Congress in Moscow. One of them, Jules Lepetit of the French CGT labour confederation, told him that the time had come for revolutionary syndicalists in the West to take a position on the problems of the revolution. The revolution had to be supported, but statist communism was not the right solution; on the contrary, it was killing the revolution; the formula of 'dictatorship of the proletariat'

was specious. (See *Le Libertaire*, 11-18 February 1921.) Jules Lepetit, disappeared along with a colleague, Marcel Vergeat, in October 1920, on his way back to France from Russia. It was suspected that his death was not an accident; it was too convenient that critics of the Bolshevik regime should have disappeared.

3   *Le Libertaire*, 25 January 1921.
4   *Le Libertaire*, 11 March 1921.
5   A translation of the agreement was printed *Le Libertaire*, 28 January 1921.
6   *Le Libertaire*, 15 April 1921. The issue of 6 May 1921 reported on the Red Labour international.

Cells in Russia[1]
'Vilkens'

When Lenin launched the slogan *All Power to the Soviets* he already knew that the latter would not be an obstacle to the action of the Communist Party. Lenin clearly had a vision, one not unlike that of the bourgeois class who use the parliamentary system to their advantage; so, in the same way, the Bolsheviks would take over the Soviet system. This foresight worked out entirely. The Bolsheviks showed just how they were thinking of using the new system, from the day following the October revolution, to the second congress of the Soviets (March 1918). Sadoul has written:

The Bolsheviks led the debate at a great speed. Scandalously, they boycotted all opposition speakers, and, from the moment they dared utter the least criticism of governmental politics, their voices were muffled by interruptions ... The way my friends the Bolsheviks got on with things was rather over the top.[2]

It wasn't enough to have a majority in the Soviets, the Party wanted to possess the soviet apparatus unconditionally, so that its directives became law throughout the country. However, the Soviet principle was entirely opposed to the interests of the Party. Communists took hold of the Soviets by force, by governmental violence (as we proved in earlier articles), installing themselves within them and refashioning them to the point that they became unrecognisable.

How did they proceed to obtain such results? The starting point was the 'Communist Cell', the minority composed of the *pure*, the *experienced* and the *clear-sighted*; and in material terms they would afterwards have a privileged position. Before

October all revolutionary elements formed a bloc, which drew the masses forwards; once in power the Bolsheviks decided that only they were exponents of the revolutionary spirit, to the exclusion of every other tendency.[3]

Soon, in the primary organisms – the factories, works, villages, etc. – the cell revealed itself as the representative of power. It became the ARGUS,⁋ the eliminator of elements that inconvenienced the party and its politics, the guide of the masses of one sort or another at election times, finally the director, the supervisor, the 'leader' in the electoral kitchen.

Anarchists did not conceive of the functioning of the Soviet system in this way; they attacked the 'cells' and they accused them of changing the very principle of the Soviets: that of free participation by the masses in affairs of a general nature.

The cells alone controlled the press, the tribune [speaking rights], they had professional propagandists in the Soviets – so their activity became easy: through such means it was not so difficult fabricate 'good elections'. Only communists were given these rights – for revolutionary reasons – and naturally, through such means, it was convenient to declare to workers and peasants that the Bolsheviks were the only revolutionary party, that all the others, including the anarchists, were petit-bourgeois, allies of the bourgeoisie, counter-revolutionaries, and that to defend the revolution, voting for the communist list was the only way. Did some people contradict all this? The Bolsheviks did not let them speak – and then who would wish to expose themselves to being called a counter-revolutionary, and of running the subsequent risk of imprisonment?

We have already seen how communists managed elections, constituting a commission, working to monopolise discussion, imposing their list. It does occasionally happen that independent persons who are not on their list obtain a majority, or that a second list is presented; in such cases the cell resorts to all sort of measures to win, they do not refrain from any sort of racketeering and cheating.

⁋ In Greek myth, an all-seeing monster.

Every list that is presented must be authorised (legalised in other words) by the signature of two communist members of the committee. If nevertheless two or more lists do confront each other, the cell's propagandists release a flood of all sorts on to their adversaries. The lies that they employ recall, point for point, those employed among bourgeois parliamentarians. If their adversaries do manage to get elected, strong-arm tactics are used and, in particular imprisonment, on the pretext of some misdemeanour, or on account of conniving with the counter-revolution. In the face of such prospects very few are ready to take the risk of presenting an opposition list. As for the mass of people, they openly display their growing lack of interest in elections. Workers and peasants see that their 'representatives' are either sectarians in their workplaces, or individuals far removed from humble workers. They readopt the habit of being governed, and, in these conditions, what events would be needed to renew the desire and a desire for *self-government*?[4]

In places where works have been closed for one reason or another the permanent committee (which looks after their upkeep) nominates, in the absence of workers, their delegates to Soviets and naturally the nominations fall on communists who, legally, represent these absentee workers.

As for that famous right to recall delegates, in practice it does not exist. On this subject, we were told that 'there was no need to make use of it, because there is always an agreement between those who are represented and representatives ...' And what would be the use of a right that cannot be freely exercised?

So, Soviets have become ossified, they have become bureaucratised and progressively routinised; they register and ensure the application of the decisions made by the central power, that is all they do now. Their activity – thus formalised and diminished – is subjected entirely to supervision by the Party, which has its active branches everywhere.

Everything is done by the Communist Party or under its management in reality, from the [highest] Council of Commissars [Sovnarkom], to the humblest village Soviet. The people know what's going on. Is some complaint to be made? It has to be addressed to power, in the same forms that are used vis-à-vis any other government. In reality, a government of bourgeois intellectuals and nobles is imposed on the people: Rakovsky, Manonilsky,** Petrovsky, Lenin, Trotsky, Lunacharsky, Chicherin, etc.

Given the conditions in which all elections are held the value of a Pan-Russian Congress of Soviets, in terms of being a representative of the labouring (producer) class is doubtful. The *Ispolkom*, the Executive Committee of the Congress, represents some sort of Senate, which in theory should control the People's Commissars, but, in reality, it limits itself to rubber stamping decrees which have already been put into operation.

By way of conclusion to these observations, one observes that the Soviet is no longer a delegation from the bottom to the top, but an apparatus subjected to top-down power; that the representatives in the Soviets arena are no longer a direct emanation of the masses, and the idea of short-term delegation, one that can be recalled at any moment exists in theory only; that executive and legislative powers reside with the Communist Party, and the latter directs the Soviets.

We should not confuse the Soviets of today with those of 1917. Earlier, Soviets were a creation of the revolutionary people; Soviets today are merely an adaption, without any life. The reality has disappeared, what remains is just a name. We, as revolutionaries, accept the original idea. This development teaches us that the system of councils should be, and should remain, entirely independent of any political party.

Wilkens voiced some criticisms of the Bolshevik government. He was arrested at 2am on 13 October and held in various prisons until 22 November. He was arrested after being accused of being an 'anarchist reformist' by Ramón Merino Garcia, a future General Secretary of the Spanish Communist Party.

** Dmitry Manuilsky?

NOTES

1. *Le Libertaire*, 29 April 1921.
2. Wilkens is quoting, in abbreviated form, a letter of 16 March 1918 from Jacques Sadoul to Albert Thomas (a French parliamentarian), in: Jacques Sadoul & Albert Thomas, *Notes sur la révolution bolchévique: octobre 1917-janvier 1919*, Paris: F. Maspéro, 1971, p. 267; available online: http://ciml.250x.com/archive/literature/french/romain_rolland/notes_sur_la_revolution_bolchevique_1917.pdf
3. The Bolsheviks set out as a goal that the Communist Party should have 'unquestioned leadership in all organisations of working people, in the unions, co-operatives, village communes, etc. The Communist Party strives especially to carry out its program and to exercise *unlimited* leadership ... Outright military discipline is needed in the party in the present epoch.' Mervyn Matthews, *Soviet Government: A Selection of Official Documents*, London: Jonathan Cape, 1974, pp. 134-5, 144.
4. Emphasis and English language in the original.

The Cheka Dictatorship[1]
'Vilkens' (Manuel Fernandez Alvar)

The dictatorship of the proletariat is exercised in Russia by the *Extraordinary Commissions*, named – in abbreviated form – as the Cheka. These commissions have tentacles extending into even the smallest village. The Cheka, originally created to destroy counter-revolutionaries, now takes on much more: the repression of speculation, deserters from the front line of the war or the workplace, supervision of offices and factories and the delivery of travel permits and passports. The remit of the Cheka is very extensive; it is at one and the same time a Committee of Public Safety, a police force and revolutionary judiciary. The Cheka also functions in the army. When a new town is taken, the first institution created is the Cheka. In the course of the offensive in Poland, a Cheka [was ready] to start work in Warsaw and marched with the [army] HQ.

The Cheka comprises commissars, examiners [prosecutors], and members of the Collegium or tribunal. It commands an armed force. Most of the commissars are young communists aged from 17 to 20; they are responsible for enquiries, investigations, surveillance and arrests. One finds among the commissars at frontier posts former Tsarist police agents; they are used as 'specialists' and are well-paid. There are many pretty young girls in place in the secret services – in hotels and other places under surveillance; they endeavour to win people's confidence to spy on what they are thinking. Many Latvian women have specialised in this line of work. Many former Tsarist magistrates have ongoing responsibilities in current tribunals. Soldiers serving the Cheka are well fed, have good accommodation, and form a chosen body. Not all of them are communists. The strictest of discipline operates among them.

The Cheka almost always arrests at night and operates in secret. Informing has become a proletarian virtue. Spies and police are everywhere; most communists belong to the Cheka – openly or secretly. Thus, the name *communist* has become a synonym for police-operative and Chekist, to the point that any peasant or a worker, before they talk to you, begin by asking: 'Are you a communist?'

If you say anything a zealous Chekist finds suspicious, in private or in public, they will denounce you. Orders will be issued to commissars. Towards two or three in the morning Chekists will arrive at your home, and you will be discretely removed by vehicle, but not without a careful search having been carried out. No one among you will be able to discover where you have been taken …

Whoever falls into the grasp of the Cheka, be they guilty or innocent, can expect to be examined before being shot (or, if they are lucky, freed). While awaiting interrogation they are moved from one prison to another [… illegible]. We have seen anarchist comrades and others arrested a year since still waiting to be interrogated. (It is one way in which, without disruption, one can be rid of unwanted people.) Cheka asylums are pretty secure, and in the end a [prisoners'] turn [for interrogation] will come around. Let us suppose that you are finally brought before an examiner: he will tell you what accusation has been made against you, and you will be submitted to his own particular form of interrogation, which proceeds without your having the services of a lawyer. He reads and has you sign his report.

Next you are sent back to prison and the examiner issues his opinion on your case. Other than the interrogation you have no defence. You are hardly in a position to refute the accusation, given that you are not told what is in your dossier. No effort is made to check facts, and even if you supply proofs, or an alibi, or cite witnesses – all that is useless. Your fate depends on the impression you have made on the examiner. His report is examined by the [Cheka] collegium which meets on Tuesdays and Fridays. This tribunal, before which you do not appear, studies the dossier, and the information from the examiner. Generally, given the number of cases, it limits itself to approving the conclusions of the examiner. In practice then, you are at the mercy of one individual, for whom any non-communist or heterodox communist is a counter-revolutionary.

Penalties vary. Decisions are not subject to appeal. The system of execution is simplified. The same evening that a tribunal ratifies a death sentence, the decision is communicated to the prisoner, and he is taken with his small belongings to a place of execution in some Cheka location.[2] At about two in the morning he is taken to a cellar. The executioner invites him to remove all his clothes (his clothes become his executioner's property). Then: 'Comrade [sic] face the wall'; 'Comrade advance'. A revolver shot into the nape of the neck, and that's it. And on to the next one. The motor of an empty van is kept running in front of the prison, while this is going on, to muffle the sounds of the shots. I asked why things were done in this way; I was told it was a way of spare the well-known sensibilities of the Russian people!

Chekists have taken their mission to heart. They have, little by little, convinced themselves that only they can defend the revolution; thus, they justify their activity and will not suffer any supervision. The real dictator of Russia is not Lenin but citizen Dzerzhinsky, the president of the Cheka of all Russia. Lenin himself gave his word to various delegates that Sasha [Alexandra] Kropotkin would have her passport; but for one reason or another the Cheka refused to let her have it.

No one in Russia can be sure that they will not fall, one day or another, into the hands of the Cheka. The Cheka decides what propaganda from every party is [allowed] or removed from circulation. It can fall on every militant and discredit them – labelling them as counter-revolutionary. And, more, the Cheka excels in the art of forging plots – an art common to all police forces. The population is terrorised by this power. The fear of denunciation has been added to the fear of famine. The trade of the police operative was odious under the Tsar, Checkists vaunt all this today and proudly sport communist insignia. The Cheka has supressed the right of asylum; whoever dares hide an escapee is condemned and subjected to the same penalties as the person he has hidden. The Cheka is never inactive; it works continually on lists of suspects, worked through in the rough and tumble of mass arrests, which it dignifies with the name of 'purges'.

I have met many insolent people, but never so many as in the Cheka. These people, given that they have the right of life and death over anyone, despise anyone who does not belong to the 'corporation' and with arrogance turn people out from their doors, treating them as slaves. The offices of the Cheka are populated by young men under the age of twenty, infatuated with their mission. They gossip, drink tea, and flirt with the young women examiners, ignoring the unhappy persons who await their decisions in cells and prisons. But it is a Chekist maxim that it is better to lock up many innocents rather than leave a counter-revolutionary at liberty. The thugs – Latvians for the most part – are well appreciated. I met one, in service to the M-Cheka of Moscow, a comrade highly esteemed by the communists who married a young girl of the former aristocracy.

Yet it is wrong to say that torture is employed by the Cheka. It executes easily, judges without guarantees, commits all sorts of injustices in the name of the proletariat, but as for torture, nothing would be so untrue. Bourgeois spies invent that. The Cheka is odious enough just as it is. It is the White[††] armies that carry out savage mutilations and executions among the communists and the people ....[3]

We do not believe that a revolution must be sweet and united, but what appears as unjustifiable and criminal is that it should be treated as an umbrella for all things, and that, using the pretext of working for the happiness of the people, the people should be forced by terror to walk down roads where

†† i.e counter-revolutionary, fascistic armies.

they do not want to go. The Bolsheviks have borrowed that from bourgeois society...[4]

NOTES

1   *Le Libertaire*, 18 March 1921.
2   The printed text has 'B-Cheka or M-Cheka'.
3   Issue 113 of *Le Libertaire* also carried brief notes on Anarchist activity since 1918.
4   *Le Libertaire*, 1 April 1921.

Rural Life[1]
'Vilkens' (Manuel Fernandez Alvar)

Generally speaking the village soviets have worked with very little due care and respect for local interests. The bureaucratic organs of the soviets, when they decided from above on how land was to be reallocated, made error after error.

In some villages peasants lamented that the division of lands was only done after the sowing season had almost finished, and that the office of land reallocation did not complete its learned deliberations [in good time]. The allocations of land were very unequal – some received all good land, others received only infertile plots; some were forced to travel between widely dispersed plots, or had to travel some distance to work on land near the homes of others. Seed would be lacking in one province, but there would be an excess in another nearby. Soviet offices took the responsibility to obtain everything; they would not allow peasants to source things themselves – except when the case was desperate and when the [sowing] season had passed.

Complicating the life of every peasant with a multitude of formalities, orders and arbitrary prohibitions – this task became the principle activity of the village soviet. The peasants survived, despite it all, but the collective spirit was lost and gave way to widespread egoism. All sorts of contraband were traded without restraint. Daily deliveries of milk, meat, eggs, cheese, flour, and other articles of everyday consumption were made by some villagers to streets and markets (despite the danger of confiscation). For the peasants Tsarist currency had twice the value of Soviet currency; they thought that if the Soviets fell, the former would be the only good money. Many of them kept a large quantity of paper roubles, but they didn't like paper money much and preferred to exchange products. In Moscow province, last year, they gave meat for bread, which they were lacking.

It is a very characteristic fact that through intermediaries, peasants have emptied city houses of everything that might make rural life more comfortable. Luxuries are to be found in the humblest of wooden shacks. In a rural cook-house we have seen all sorts of pretty furniture, such as valuable silk divans. Currently, in cottages, one can find magnificent mirrors, pianos and gramophones, above all gramophones which peasants greatly like, and which are placed in the place of honour before a visitor. Peasants work with golden rings on their fingers, others walk in the village with shoes with high heels, and hard sun-hats. One day an anarchist comrade locked up in the Butyrka prison received from his partner a card telling him: 'Now peasants are coming with flour, and since I have nothing with which to pay them I have chosen the clock, your suit and shoes [with which to pay them]; so now we have flour for another month ...'

Just now, anyone looking for fine things should go to the country. Cities are emptied of everything. Anything manufactured disappears as soon as it is made. Workers, speculators, etc., travel to areas far from the cities to find produce, peasants have no need to molest them. On the outskirts of the stations, where there are small markets, peasants sell all sorts of products; prices vary from place to place.

Despite their relative prosperity, peasants have too many worries to be happy. The Ukraine itself – once one of the most comfortable places in the whole world – has come to resemble a graveyard.

One must be careful not to make hasty critical judgements about peasants. War and revolution have made for a deep transformation in their psychology. Broad horizons do not intimidate them. Moreover, the Russian peasant is a part of a young people, one which has a future and a lively and all-embracing spirit. They can understand things clearly and assimilate new ideas and they find in communism in particular, something that chimes with their own customs.

We have observed the moral effect that has been produced by government clumsiness, and the criticism that is being made by peasants – for the most part with good sense and with justice on their side. For some time now they have believed they have rights. They say that the revolution should also serve themselves and not just the Bolsheviks.

When we travelled from Kharkov to Kiev, Antonov, the commissar general for the Ukraine, occupied a special wagon. [We met him] when we arrived at Barachala station, where the train stopped for the night, and a big meeting was held by lamplight. Interruptions and negative comments arose on all sides from beginning to end and Antonov was not heard much. One very old man explained that peasants were not refusing to provide supplies for the Red Army, that is to say for their sons and daughters, but they were disgusted by the hundreds of soldiers who were in the villages doing nothing. As for the city people, they did not demand manufactured goods to the value of their products – but what they did want above all was better tools and seeds to make and preserve a better harvest.

'You can see that we have neither salt nor hay for this winter. Give us these things and the means to replace them. In return, we will give everything you ask for.'

'If we do not have salt to give you that is because of Makhno', replied Antonov.

'But,' [they replied,] Makhno is in Ekaterinoslav [...] Poltava, whereas the salt-works are in Kherson. And we cannot even obtain permission to go and obtain some for ourselves.'

The Russian peasant is far from being a simpleton. They like to bargain and they know how to. It is interesting to see how great the desire for education is in the countryside. Most villages have someone better educated who teaches others. Young members of the former bourgeoisie have become teachers. There is a great passion for reading. Books have a great value as a medium of exchange. One can see young peasants on a cottage doorstep passing hours together reading books. Naturally easy works, novels – mainly works of Tolstoy, Turgenev, Dostoyevsky, Gogol – have a great readership. Histories of revolution and travel tales, are well thumbed by peasants. Daily papers are read avidly, one peasant in front of me gave half a dozen eggs to read an issue of *Izvestia*. *Izvestia* means *Notices,* and *Pravda* means *Truth*. And the peasants say with some spirit: 'There are no notices in *Truth*, no truth in *Notices*.'

Peasants are interested in the circumstances of peasants abroad, they asked us why no peasants had come as delegates to the [second] congress of the Communist International; they would like to know about conditions on the land and the life of peasants in Latin countries, and they asked us why there was no revolutions [among us].

As for religion, the changes brought about by the revolution boil down to very little. Peasants have preserved their admirable faith, they feed and venerate their priests, esteem icons and sing in church services. Such things are not peculiar to villages, since we have plainly seen processions in Moscow streets, churches are full at all hours there; the priests get on well, they are respected by the Bolsheviks – they fear the power of religion and of its ministers.

To sum up, we believe that the Russian peasants are for the most part revolutionary in feeling and instinct; they distrust counter-revolutionaries, monarchists, republicans, democrats and reformists, but their independent and free spirit prevents them for seeking new bosses. For this reason, and in general, the Bolsheviks, if they had followed other policies, would not have met with hostility. The peasants, however, do not want to accept that the revolution should end up with a regime of oppression and terror, of economic and political authoritarianism, denying peasant feelings and interests.

In an earlier issue of *Le Libertaire*,[2] Vilkens noted that peasants had taken the land for themselves. They wanted land ownership, not just the right to use land and feared that if the current regime was defeated they would lose it. Vilkens had encountered anarchist-communist co-ops in the Volga region; these would appear to have worked well and harmoniously, without priests or police.

The Bolsheviks had attempted to set up rural Soviet enterprises – much like factories. Relations between the peasant and the state had deteriorated and peasants passively resisted. Peasants produced food only for themselves and, where they were able to, sold through [illegal] commercial markets. Consequently, Soviet warehouses received only a third of what they might have expected. The lack of animal feed caused peasants to kill animals that could not be fed over the winter.

'The situation became untenable, and at the congress of the Communist Party last March the Bolsheviks were forced by necessity to change their peasant policy radically. They established taxes in kind, leaving peasants the freedom to dispose of their surpluses, in other words complete freedom of commerce.

This change of policy was inevitable, and the error was that they had not understood these things earlier. Through this vast experience of failure, the idea of communism has been greatly diminished in the eyes of the masses; it was lamentable that things should have come to such a pass. This lamentable consequence might have been avoided if there had not been obstinate attempts to establish a barrack-room communism.'[3]

NOTES

1 *Le Libertaire*, 16 July 1921; *La Antorcha*, 25 November 1921.
2 *Le Libertaire*, 10 June 1921.
3 Ibid., conclusion.

The Revolution in 1920 – Nine Points[1]
'Vilkens' (Manuel Fernandez Alvar)

This text was the first in a series, 'Six months in Russia'[2] published as in *Le Libertaire*, in 1921.[3]

The author 'Vilkens', had visited many cities – including Kharkhov, Kiev, Moscow, St. Petersburg, and Poltava – in the latter half of 1920. He had also travelled in rural areas under various guises and met workers, peasants and anarchists, as well as high officials – including Lenin.[4] He was very briefly a soldier in the Red Army and spent some weeks in prison.

Vilkens came to believe that revolutionary opinion was being misled about the course of events in Russia. He sought to verify the official information he had been given. He thought visitors coming to Russia in 1920 for the second congress of the Communist International might be taken in.[5] One German communist – staying in a hotel – ate ample white bread and reported that people ate as much bread as they wanted. Outside the hotels serving foreign delegates many Russian people were starving; they had seen no white bread since the revolution, the black bread that was available was often inedible.[6] Vilkens wrote: go see things for yourself – I am not misleading you.[7]

1. There may have been a day when the Bolsheviks represented revolutionary aspirations, but today all that is finished. It would be wrong to believe that the Russian Revolution and the Bolsheviks are the same thing.

2. That the Communist Party and those that it endows are walking rapidly towards the establishment of a class with [distinct] interests opposed to the interests of the revolutionary masses.

3. That the proletarian dictatorship is an instrument of oppression in the hands of a new class, [and] this class is not controlled by the proletariat and is antagonistic towards it.

4. That the [new] regime uses terror even more than the Tsarist regime, because it finds it more difficult to supress people who have seen and recognised the light of revolution.

5. That the Russian Communists and the Communists of the entire world make war on capital to establish a so-called proletarian STATE, which, with all its bureaucracy, is the realisation of Marx's thinking, and while it breaks the shackles of capitalism it places new chains on the shoulders of the proletariat.

6. That the formula labelled 'Dictatorship of the Proletariat' puts an end to the participation of the masses in current activity, for the benefit of the State.

Consequentially we know that:

a. The will of the labouring (productive) people is less well represented in the Soviet regime than in parliamentary regimes in bourgeois countries.

b. The Russian trade unions are unions only in name, like Soviets, they are simple an appendage of the bureaucracy.

c. The true revolutionaries, principally the anarchists, who wish to defend the conquests of the revolution are persecuted, imprisoned and shot without legal process.

d. That the Red Army has ceased to be a revolutionary army. Having taken on the character of a regular army, it will tomorrow perhaps be yellow and after tomorrow perhaps white. That a military regime that would be established on such a basis would be the greatest peril for the revolution.

e. that [the watchwords] *the factories to the workers, homes for tenants, mines to the workers*, etc, have sunk into the limbo of oblivion.

7. That the plagues of capitalist regimes – prostitution, theft, favouritism, elections – flourish and affect Russia as much as bourgeois countries.

8. That one should not be misled by the reforms that have been made in Russia: some exist on paper, others benefit the privileged classes, and the greater part of them, those that have a philanthropic character, are even exceeded by other advanced capitalist countries.

9. That the blockade of the Entente is the most monstrous crime, because all its repercussions are paid for by the [Russian] people. And, if the imperialist bandits think that this will make the people revolt they are greatly in error. The entire Russian people stands ready to fight anyone who would violate Russian land, or who would intervene in its internal affairs which have nothing to do with them.

And, to finish, a conclusion: The Russian revolution proves undeniably, against the opinion of reformists, that the capitalist class is not needed at all, that it is a parasite that society can do without. And here we are in agreement with the communists, except that the latter wish to impose a transitional regime which will make them the profiteers of the revolution while we do not expect anything for our own particular benefit and fight for the people themselves to benefit from the revolution.

NOTES

1 Our title, the text has been very slightly abridged; from *Le Libertaire*, 14 January 1921.
2 The series was published between in *Le Libertaire* from January to July 1921. Other than the articles translated here there were others addressing various issues, for example: 'With Lenin in the Kremlin'; 'A visit with Kropotkin'; 'Bolsheviks, Anarchists and Kibalchich'; 'The politics of trade union Internationalism'; 'Education'.
3 The series was republished in the Argentinean newspaper *La Antorcha*.
4 Vilkens met Lenin in September 1920; see *Le Libertaire*, 11 February 1921; *La Antorcha*, 1 April 1921. Many of these texts are available online in Spanish, e.g. http://www.antorcha.net/index/hemeroteca/periodico_antorcha/1921/2.pdf

5   Vilkens was probably in touch with the national committee of the CNT. (Jason Garner, *El Primer Exilio. Los libertarios españoles en Francia antes de la Segunda República*, http://www.academia.edu/11181022/El_primer_exilio._Los_libertarios_espa%C3%B1oles_en_Francia_antes_de_la_Segunda_Republica). In Moscow, he met with delegates attending the second Congress of the Communist International.
6   *Le Libertaire*, 21 January 1921.
7   *Le Libertaire*, 1 April 1921.

Encounters[1]
Ángel Pestaña Núñez

Pestaña was in Russia from 26 June to 6 September as a delegate from the Spanish Labour Confederation (CNT) to the congress of the Communist International.

We visited a communist agricultural farm in Saratov (here in Spain we might call it a state farm). We were hoping to see some real communism.

We were able to discover a little about its organisation. The 'Communist Colony' was an old farm owned by one of the richest landowners in the region. The Saratov Soviet took it over after the revolution, appointing a director and an agronomic expert. Permanent workers had a wage of two thousand roubles a month and the *payok* (the standard ration). The casual workers received rations and 75 roubles daily.

Workers were expected to work eight hours a day – as in any industrial enterprise. The director could dismiss them whenever he saw fit, without giving any explanation, and with only eight days' notice. Shocked by this comment, I told Lozovsky[2] that there was nothing communist about such arrangements, and that it was no different from any other enterprise we had seen previously. But he insisted it was a communist experiment. I was perplexed by this answer and by this experiment in communist organisation. And keep in mind that in order to visit the 'Communist Colony' and to get to know how it was organised, we had had to travel about twenty kilometres in a truck, down almost impassable tracks.

The gala receptions never stopped in Saratov. It ranked as a key population centre; it was an industrial centre of some importance and a transport hub for a region very rich in cereals and all sorts of produce. There were visits to government offices, military parades, visits to various factories and industries; there were speeches, meetings, tea. The familiar refrain of the *Internationale* sounded off constantly in every city, we were never without it.

The two days we spent in Saratov were lively and useful. We were disappointed in one thing only: that the people – real people – (not the people who played parts as extras or in the choirs for our visits, receptions and meetings) might also have really intervened in the celebrations, and taken a part in the proclamations of contentment and joy that appeared to accompany us.

As I said above, we left the Volga in Saratov, with great sadness for my part, and took the train, the same one that had brought us from Moscow to Nizhny-Novgorod, which had been sent to Saratov for us. At night, a day later, we took the train for Tula. There were still some days before the Congress opened, so we were in no hurry to get back to Moscow. We chose to visit Tula.

Tula also is an industrial centre of some importance. It has military industries and makes samovars. We visited a munitions factory. The workers there were convinced and bitter anti-Bolsheviks. Three months before our visit they had gone on a strike and lost.[3] The Bolsheviks imposed vicious terms when they returned to work. They condemned thirty-five strikers, those they called ringleaders, to terms of imprisonment of one to eight years. It should be pointed out – always in the interest of fullest impartiality and so that readers' judgment is not distorted – that the sentences passed on these strikers at the Tula munitions factories should not be taken at face value, or as a stick with which to beat the Bolsheviks. We must plainly say that although to us the penalties imposed by the Soviet seemed harsh and disproportionate, the strike was unjustified; furthermore at that moment it had counter-revolutionary consequences.

Tula munitions workers, even under the Tsars, enjoyed benefits and privileges not enjoyed by workers elsewhere. And these privileges were respected by the Soviet Government, inasmuch as it was appropriate and possible, given the range of wages and working conditions that obtained for other workers. So, enjoying these privileges, and being in a superior position as compared to other workers all over Russia, what could justify a call to strike? Moreover, there was another factor that made the circumstances of this strike all even more tragic.

The Tula munitions factories are, as I have said, the most important ones in all Russia, that is to say that they are the only factories that manufacture cartridges, bayonets and small arms for the army, and they were the sole suppliers of these war materials. Workers decided to declare a strike and stage a conflict in these workshops at the very moment when the whole world was anticipating the threat of a Polish invasion of Russia. Such a strike would leave the Red Army defenceless against the enemy, would it not? We would have to say that at such a moment strikes would always be inappropriate. Since these workers' conditions were better than that of all other workers in Soviet Russia there could be no justification for their demands for improvements. On the other hand, the declaration of a strike might have led to an invasion by reactionary armies.

True, one might view the penalties imposed on the thirty-five workers thought to be ringleaders of the strike as excessive; but their conduct, like that of their comrades, was neither sensible not appropriate. The commander-in-chief of that sector of the Red Army and of the forces that guarded and then suppressed the strike at these munitions plants was an anarchist, a member of one of the existing anarchist groups. We wanted to speak to him; but since he couldn't speak French properly, and we couldn't speak Russian or English, which were the languages he spoke, we were prevented from asking him any questions about what had really happened.

Thanks, however, to a local young man who spoke good French, we were nonetheless able to exchange thoughts about the situation in the country. We realised immediately, from the way this young man spoke, that we were dealing with someone who was not well disposed to Bolshevism or the revolution itself. We could see that his views suffered from the same degree of partiality as those of the government officials and government sympathisers – but from quite the opposite perspective.

He confirmed the views I had formed regarding how we were seen by the people we visited – the Russian people, the people of the villages and cities. He said that we were just a handful of individuals purchased in Europe by the Bolsheviks and paid splendidly, cast to appear as delegates from the socialists and communists of the world. And that was why the people kept their distance from us and laughed privately at the farce these oddities represented. This view was later confirmed by many people I visited in Moscow. It was, then, no invention of this speaker – it was a truth – and one that most or all people believed quite absolutely. Since we still had some time, we travelled on from Tula to Ivanovo-Voznesensk, a famous centre of the textile industry, known as the Russian Manchester.

To avoid tedious repetition, we shall omit a description of the official receptions, which were also quite stupendous. We had opportunities to speak with all sorts of officials in the office of the city Soviet, and we asked questions about the region's economic and political situation.

'The economy,' they told us, 'is very bad'. Of the hundreds of textile factories that exist in the city and the province, barely twenty are functioning, and even these are not working intensively. Most textile workers have had to leave, and take other jobs if they can find anything, or, lacking resources, they suffer greatly from hunger and poverty.' As for politics, the members of the Soviet boasted that Ivanovo-Voznesensk as one of the most solid bastions of Bolshevism.

'It was here, in our city,' we were told, 'that the first Russian Soviet was formed in 1905, in that great revolutionary movement. We took the initiative to create one, even though no political party had resolved to do so. Various comrades from this Soviet have now been appointed to preside over the Soviets of several other important parts of Russia, including Saratov. This is proof that the party has confidence in us; we comply with their orders, and demonstrate equal loyalty.'

In response to one of our questions, concerning whether the Bolshevik elements were predominant in 1905 in Ivanovo, they answered no – at that time, Mensheviks and Social Revolutionaries were dominant. 'Even quite recently,' they said, 'they were in the majority here, in the revolutions of March and November of 1917; but the communist party has delivered us from them. Some have become communists; others have gone away. We are very harsh with these counter-revolutionaries.'

That night we left Ivanovo-Voznesensk and at 11 a.m. on the following day, 14 July, we arrived in Moscow. In the fourteen days of our trip, we had covered hundreds of kilometres, we had visited Russian cities, villages and hamlets, we had participated in more than thirty rallies and had seen the tremendous defects of communist centralisation and some of the fundamental errors of Russian communism.

But what impressed me most was my visit to the kindergarten in Simbirsk.

When I was there, I was told that it was only *communists'* children who had a right to benefit from kindergartens, because their parents were the ones who made the revolution. The spectre of the bourgeoisie came to me – the vision came so fast that it was impossible for me to ever forget it. These parents were as cruel and miserly, or even more cruel, than those who had been overthrown, and always more concerned with the necessity of establishing their own power, because they were new on the scene. How I would have preferred to have been mistaken! How I would have preferred that this could be nothing but the workings of a fevered imagination, driven by the prejudice that might influence me driven by life under capitalism!

I must also mention the public marketplace near the docks in Simbirsk, where all kinds of commercial transactions took place, in money and in kind. The traders were inhabitants of that region, and mostly Muslims. The market sold everything. Not in great abundance; but everything. I bought myself some country sandals and paid eight thousand roubles, and they were the cheapest. You could find anything in this weekly market: bread, flour, meat, dry vegetables, hardware and haberdashery; but the most abundant things were clothes and especially shoes.

Let me repeat, once and for all, that the filth and abandon we saw on the streets of Petrograd and barely glimpsed in Moscow were clearly visible wherever we went. In Saratov things were indescribably bad, piles of refuse and rubbish of every sort were everywhere. Some streets were more or less impassable, such was the stench. Some groups of delegates, having barely turned down a street, were forced to immediately turn around and retreat, so bad was the stench and the fetid pong that they emitted. It would have been impossible to live there if the streets had not been so narrow and the houses so small (of one or two floors at the highest).

Many houses were in a ruinous condition, or looked as if they might collapse, because without materials, no repairs could be made. Because of this lack many families were forced to live in small spaces crowded together. Also, because many houses had been confiscated by the local Soviets, and people were not allowed to live in them, and because permission from the local Soviet to live in these houses could not be had, and the price was outrageous.

We were most interested to discover if people were eager to learn how to read and write; we were told they were, although the results obtained so far were not as spectacular as in Moscow or Petrograd. The majority, tormented by a lack of food, forced to scrounge for their daily nourishment, had little concern for culture. The very human desire to preserve one's own existence outweighed the merits of cultural improvement.

One further very interesting observation: never once did we see a drunk on the streets, everyone knows how much damage alcoholism has inflicted on Russia; this is one victory that Bolshevism can celebrate.

NOTES

1. Our Title. This text, and the next one, are taken from *Setenta días en Rusia. Lo que yo vi*, Barcelona: Tipografía Cosmos, 1924, pp. 53-59. The original Spanish text can be found here: http://www.saber.es/web/biblioteca/libros/setenta-dias-rusia/setenta-dias-rusia.pdf A translation is available on the Libcom website: https://libcom.org/files/Seventy%20days%20in%20Russia%20What%20I%20saw%20-%20Angel%20Pesta%C3%B1a.pdf
2. Solomon Lozovsky, 1878–1952, was a prominent Bolshevik trade union official.
3. There is an account of the strike, which began on 6 June, in Jonathan Aves, *Workers Against Lenin*, London: Tauris, 1996, pp. 50-56. Workers were angered by compulsory Sunday working, by the replacement of shop committees; they wanted better food, and were concerned with abuses in the rationing system.

Factory Committees[1]
Ángel Pestaña Núñez

The extract below[2] discusses relationships between workers, factory committees, trade unions and management, as seen by Pestaña, three years into the revolution.[3] Pestaña had interviewed several trade union officials, this text presents a compilation of questions and answers.

And the factory committee: who designates it?
The workers in each factory.

And who suggests the list of candidates? Are workers free to choose whoever they want?
Nothing like that. A list of names is always provided by the local Soviet, or by members of the Communist Party working in the factory. The list is final. Names may not be deleted.

So, within these norms, no one, unless they are a communist can be elected onto the factory committees.
No, sometimes non-party persons are included on the lists.

And what are the factory committee's responsibilities?
It is a personification of the government and the trade unions. It exercises vigilance, it ensure that workers work, that they are sufficiently productive; it fixes wage rates; it imposes penalties and fines on the workers who do not pull their weight; it fires those who do not meet expectations; it requests new workers for the factory from the labour exchange; it classifies workers by category; it guards against wasting raw materials; it receives

workers' demands; it serves as an intermediary between workers, the director and management; it prepares factory elections, and, finally it maintains order and discipline, promotes efficiency and everything else that makes things work smoothly.

Can workers request the removal of one or all members of the factory committee?

Yes, of course. Anyone who has a responsible post may recalled, it follows that any representative may be dismissed by those they represent.

How do the workers go about sacking a representative?

They ask the factory committee to call a meeting and when the committee agrees, they meet. They present their grievances there, the factory committee receives them and transmits them onwards, to the trade union committee, which examines them and proceeds as it sees fit.

But this is a contradiction! The workers have to request permission to hold a meeting from the very persons they want to get rid of. The latter – those who are the subject of the complaints, have to register that complaint and pass it on, without the least intervention from those who submitted it. If this is how things are done successful demands [for sacking managers] must be very rare!

Yes, very rare. It almost never happens. But you should understand party discipline, it requires that a factory committee that has been petitioned by the workers seeking to sack it is obliged to tell the trade union of the wishes of the workers that it represents.

Good; but you have to consider personal self-interest as against party discipline. Never ever is there any desire to see someone removed, many things prove as much. And besides that, there are all the bureaucratic procedures you would have to go through, the fear of reprisals, the presence of the Cheka at every meeting, the fact that there is no press in which abuses and arbitrary acts might be publicised, and the fear of being labelled a counter-revolutionary –

FACTORY COMMITTEES

all these things smother protest and any thought of rebellion. And members of the factory committee: how long is their term?

Six months.

May they be re-elected?

Yes.

Once a factory committee has been chosen, are members considered as workers or State employees, in respect of wages and rations? Are they obliged to do [factory] work or are they exempt from any labouring?

The members of the factory committee, once they have been designated, cease to be considered as workers and are considered to belong to the category of State employees. They have no obligation to work; if they do, they do so voluntarily. Their mission is surveillance, to ensure others do work.

So, they become workplace police of a sort.

That is a rather harsh word. They have none of the attributes of a police force. We have already described their role.

And when a worker has been vexed by a factory committee person or given a lower wage rate than the one he* thinks he deserves, what procedures does he have to follow or how would he have to proceed to make the trade union take up that claim? – Because one assumes that trade unions should be concerned to defend organised workers in such cases.

Of course, trade unions attend to workers in such cases and defend and protect them. If a worker's rights are disregarded, or if he has been assigned to a lower wage category than the one which he believes he should have, he goes to the factory committee and submits his complaint in writing. The factory committee then forwards the complaint, always following proper channels, to the Local Committee of the Trade Union, which in turn sends it to the Executive Committee of the Trade Union to which the plaintiff belongs. Once the Executive

---

* The author uses masculine forms.

Committee of the Trade Union has ruled, for or against, the same channels through which the complaint has passed on its way to the Executive Committee of the Trade Union are used to pass it back to its source. Sometimes a newly-elected member will receive a verdict regarding a complaint against a predecessor – because factory committee members, are elected only for a six-month term and not longer, (although they are often re-elected). In such a case the new committee must give satisfaction to the worker concerned, if the claim is accepted, or deny him in the opposite case. That is often the result. But you must not overlook the difficulty that one factory committee has when it comes to resolving a dispute that arose even before it was elected. The faults or shortcomings of the one should not be paid for by the next committee.

Of course, but as to the worker who was personally wronged or has lost pay after being assigned to a lower wage category than that to which he was entitled to: who would compensate him or give him redress? The rights of a worker who has been wronged should not to be given any less respect than the rights of the factory committee. Within a communist regime, where power is exercised in the name of the working class, it is only right that workers should have justice. He shouldn't have privilege, but he should have justice.

And that is just what happens. There is not a single complaint, submitted by a worker, that does not get attention.

We do not deny that, but we do deny that this attention is effective. First of all, because there are so many stages which things must go through, and because there is no option for a worker to set things in motion; secondly, because the complaint must be judged without his being heard [in person], which is the most important thing. The Executive Committee of the Trade Union, in order to preserve the prestige of the factory committee and of the Communist Party, through which it is represented in the workplace, will always decide things in their favour. Hence the few successful recall actions against committees and the fact that the workers are not interested in them.

On the contrary. The workers are extremely interested in the factory committee.

Even communist workers deny that [workers are extremely interested in the factory committee]. As for other workers and what interests them, we doubt what you say. Finally, we left it at that.

Vilkens was aware of Pestaña's critical perspectives on the development of management in Russia and on the subordination of Russia's trade unions. Vilkens concluded: 'We are persuaded that many syndicalists from various lands, those who are not shackled to the Communist Party, being aware that it would be impossible in the foreseeable future for syndicalism to follow the Bolsheviks' injunctions, will realise the necessity of a Revolutionary Syndicalist International, independent of political parties old and new and based on Federalism and Autonomy.'[4]

NOTES

1 Our title.
2 This text is taken from *Setenta días en Rusia. Lo que yo vi*, Barcelona: Tipografía Cosmos, 1924, pp. 87-90.
3 In 1917 factory committees functioned through mass assemblies of workers held in working time, the imposition of 'iron discipline' in the spring of 1918 was a big step in the destruction of this mass participatory democracy, henceforward assemblies met when sanctioned, and outside working time.
4 *Le Libertaire*, 5 June 1921.

A Meeting with Victor Serge[1]
Armando Borghi

Armando Borghi represented the Italian Syndicalist Union (USI) at the congress of the 'Red' Labour Union International, in July 1920. His journey home from Moscow was interrupted by a spell of imprisonment – a frequent occurrence for many delegates in transit to and from Russia. The USI eventually decided not to participate in the 'Red' Labour Union International; instead it joined the revived International Workers' Association which brought together a range of radical and syndicalist unions in Europe and the Americas. On his return to Italy Borghi had told Errico Malatesta, and his partner, Virgilia D'Andrea that 'between us and the Bolsheviks the distance is astronomical'.[2]

Victor Serge* was at one time an anarchist individualist. He first writings appeared under the pen name of le Rétif (The Agitated),[3] his real name was Victor-Napoléon Lvovich Kibalchich. Borghi had first met Serge in Paris, in 1912. Serge spent much of the First World War in Barcelona. Later he travelled to Russia and served under Zinoviev in the Communist International. The exchange below might suggest that Serge was concerned that he might be betrayed if his conversations were reported back to his masters, and that unpleasant consequences might have followed.

Serge criticised both anarchist and communist politics. Gaston Leval (see the following selection), suggests that Serge was insincere and duplicitous. There is something about Serge that lends itself to this accusation: his espousal first of

---

* Born in Brussels in 1890, died in Mexico, 1947.

individualist anarchist and later of Bolshevism, and his ability to slip across political divides. It would perhaps be kinder to say that Serge was attracted to some form of democratic socialism, but did not get very far in elaborating a clear position. By the early 1920s most anarchists had concluded that the hopes they had placed in Bolshevik Russia were misplaced; Serge did not join them. His criticism of the repression of the Kronstadt rising, was publicised only in 1937; it earned him vicious rebuke from Trotsky.[4]

An anarchist visitor, coming from Italy, that was a great rarity. Such a person was to be passed from one official to another – and always under the careful eye of an interpreter. Old militants who had once taken refuge in France and Italy came, one by one, to talk to me about the prospects for immanent revolution in Italy. Among them, I met Victor Serge, alias Kibalchich. We recalled our meeting in Paris in 1912. He had been an anarchist and he had passed through hard times for secondary action around the fringes of the Bonnot gang.[†] He was now a member of the Bolshevik Party. Being alone for a brief moment, he made an appointment with me for the following day.

The next day I knocked on his door – a Spanish comrade was with me. Victor Serge, half-opened the door and asked me: 'How can I help you?' Somewhat amazed, I reminded him that the previous day we had agreed to meet. Seeming even more astonished than me, he told me that I had misunderstood, and furthermore, he was just about to go out to take care of some important business. It was hard to swallow. I retraced my journey. When I arrived back in my room, the telephone rang.

'Who's speaking?'

'It's me, Serge.'

'So, have you changed your mind?'

[†] The Bonnot gang seized money using arms and vehicles in Paris in 1911-12. Serge was sentenced to imprisonment for robbery. The gang were associated with the magazine *L'Anarchie*. This sort of individualist anarchism was repudiated by the Fédération révolutionnaire communiste / Fédération communiste anarchiste (Anarchist-Communist Federation).

'Are you alone?'
'So, come over at once.'
'So, I was right?'
'No ... yes, but come over anyway, I'll explain.'
I went back, he wasn't expecting me to ask questions. 'Listen my dear, I gave you an appointment, for us *alone*,'
'But that Spaniard is a comrade.' I said.
'I understand – you, you have come from Europe.'[5] And having said that, he went through a rosary: The Soviets have been swallowed up by the Communist Party. The leaders use them as means of spying. Any dissent is a betrayal, and every betrayal has to be met with some 'elimination'. In the factories, the disciplinary system is ruthless. Trotsky is a perfect tyrant. There is neither communism here, nor socialism, nor anti-communism, but Prussian military discipline ... He had remained an anarchist, but what would have been the use committing suicide by working in an opposition that would be worth less than nothing? No one would have understood. No one would have followed. No one would have known. He would have only have been taken for a spy ... This was the horrible logic of totalitarianism.[6]

Armando Borghi spoke at a congress of the Italian Anarchist Union in November 1921 and reported back on his trip to Russia.[7]

NOTES

1   Our title, from: Armando Borghi, *Mezzo secolo di anarchia (1898-1945)*, Catania: Edizioni Anarchismo, 1989, p. 235.
2   Ibid., p. 252.
3   Rirette Maîtrejean, *Souvenirs d'anarchie*, Quimperlé: La Digitale, 2005, pp. 27ff.
    http://www.lelibertaire.xyz/Rirette-maitrejean-souvenirs-anarchie.pdf
4   These matters are documented in David Cotterill, Ed., *The Serge-Trotsky Papers*, London: Pluto Press, 1994. Some of Serge's last writings are in *Le nouvel imperialisme russe*, Paris: Spartacus, 1972.
5   Perhaps Serge was aware of the experience of Wilkens – Wilkens had

reported that his imprisonment in Russia followed on from his being denounced by a Spanish delegate, Ramón Merino Garcia. *Le Libertaire*, l8-25 February 1921; Wayne Thorpe, *'The Workers Themselves'*: *revolutionary syndicalism and international labour, 1913-1923*, Dordrecht: Kluwer, 1989, p. 303.

6   These views would seem to contrast with those he expressed in August 1920, in a letter to the comrades of *Le Libertaire* and others. Serge argued: 'As regards means, the hard necessities of revolution *left us no choice*. Everything was forced on us, and was done by the Communist Party, and we had to be a part of it, *failing which we would have been against it, and with reaction.*' (Emphasis added). From: https://www.marxists.org/francais/serge/works/1920/08/anarchistes.htm Gaston Leval criticised this binary, 'either/or' approach: 'In truth, and without denying in any way the consequences of the civil war, these accusations against other fractions were nothing more than lies. The fact that one does not submit to one minority faction does not categorically imply that these other currents are formed or 'traitors', 'counter-revolutionaries', 'liquidators' or 'Philistines'. Gaston Leval, *Lenin: Sepulturero de la Revolucion Rusa*, (https://laturbaediciones.files.wordpress.com/2010/03/lenin.pdf). *Le Libertaire* of 4 March 1921 printed a letter from Serge, and reply. The reply said Serge should be ashamed. How could Serge demand that his words be published abroad, when, in Russia, anarchists were 'cruelly silenced' by the regime he supported? The polemic continued, for example in Gastón Leval, 'Replica a Victor Serge', *La Protesta* (Suplemento), 26 June 1922. One can find Serge's later perspectives in: *Memoirs of a Revolutionary*, New York: New York Review of Books, 2012, in *Destiny of a Revolution*, London: Jarrolds, 1937; and online: https://www.marxists.org/archive/serge/index.htm

7   See: *Umanità Nova*, 8 November 1921. This edition had a report on debates on Russia at the Third congress of Italian Anarchist Union. Borghi is reported to have said that the journey to Russia was made in the hope of uniting non-parliamentary parties on a national and an international level, to hasten the revolution, and with the intention of joining the Third International. An accord with Russia, or with the Third International had reason to exist only if in consequence there was an accord between the various Italian vanguard parties. In Russia, one became convinced of antagonisms that were not so evident in Italy. The Bolsheviks were unscrupulous opportunists, and statists: for a time, the Bolsheviks had allied themselves with anarchists against Menshevik influence; later they turned on anarchists. The congress voted a resolution in line with these ideas, mentioning solidarity with Russian anarchists and calling for press freedom and freedom of assembly and

organisation. (*Tutto per la rivoluzione rusa, ma decisamente contro il governo dittatoriale* – All for the Russian Revolution, but decisively against the dictatorial government). http://bibliotecaborghi.org/wp/wp-content/uploads/2016/01/UN_1921_n179.pdf This issue reported also on a lecture given by Borghi on the 5 November. (See also *Umanità Nova* of 27 October.)

IMPRESSIONS OF RUSSIA[1]
Gaston Leval

Gaston Leval arrived in Russia in June 1921 and returned to Spain some four months later. He was a delegate for the Spanish National Labour Confederation (the CNT)[2] and attended meetings of the 'Red' Labour Union International and the Communist International. He worked to secure the release of anarchists imprisoned in Russia. Much of his writings on Russia concerned the situation and treatment of imprisoned Anarchists (and other socialists). He and others met with Trotsky and discussed – with some acrimony – the release of prisoners[3] as well as the role of trade union bureaucracies in Russia and elsewhere. Leval joined a delegation that met with Lenin to solicit the release of prisoners.

Leval noted that some persons were particularly attracted to the task of using force to destroy existing institutions – in the name of general interests – and they were also ready to impose themselves on others if that was necessary, even within their own organisations, from which they drew their inspiration. While he admitted the necessity of using force, Leval commented that this force was a means and not an end. Revolution that was only destructive led nowhere. Professionalisation in the use of armed force 'is the most dangerous of specialisations' – as for example with the Cheka.[4]

... Another train took us on to Petrograd. My first thought was to find Victor Serge.[5] ... Victor Serge was known – but not liked – by some the Spaniards, these men of the people were displeased by his aristocratic ways, and the rare way he played with his fine, elegant, distinguished hands. I only found this out later. But I knew, before I left, that among French comrades who admired his intelligence, there was some disdain for a man who lacked the courage needed to face life's difficulties and make the effort to adapt to work. He hadn't persisted with typesetting, a semi-skilled trade which Spanish comrades had found for him (he had learnt a little typography in prison). He and his partner quickly disposed of the funds raised for him in France. He seemed without hope, incapable of dealing with the challenges he had had to face. Trying to make him change his mind, and seeking to provoke what I thought was a healthy reaction I had suggested he should leave with me and travel around Spain. He lacked the confidence, and perhaps also physical strength for the adventure. One day he did return to France, his expulsion decree notwithstanding.

… Victor Serge failed to find a way of living and was unable to get himself accepted as a volunteer in the French army. Doubtless he remained an enemy of war, as the articles he published in *Tierra y Libertad* show. And yet, there he was wanting to enlist and go to the front. What was the reason for such contradictions? In my view, he was plainly beside himself, and was looking for some indirect suicide.[6] Next, other signed articles of his appeared in some of the anarchist press. Now this sometime individualist declared himself a defender of the Russian revolution, in its Bolshevik Marxist form. All of this seemed mad to me, but he had suffered a lot, and someone who has suffered should be not be judged quite like others. I said as much to Alphonse, but he was always lacking in understanding for certain human problems.

These negative facts didn't undermine my admiration for him. I remembered a man of brimming intelligence, a fine reporter, a brilliant talker. His propaganda in favour of the Bolshevik dictatorship[7] made no impression on me at all, but one couldn't be honest like me and keep one's reputation.*

---

* Leval appears to be implying that one couldn't be a journalist, be published in the Bolshevik press and retain one's integrity.

All the same, the interview I had in company with Arlandis,[†] amazed me. Everything that Victor Serge told us 'in confidence' (being convinced that, given our friendship, we would not betray him) contradicted what was affirmed, or what one might infer, from his writings.

As for the Cheka – the mother of the GPU, the grandmother of the NKVD, and the great-grandmother of the NVD – he declared: it is an institution which at first rendered great services but it has become very inconvenient; it is now so strong that no one knows how to get rid of it. About the Communist Party: more and more it is being invaded by revolutionary opportunists (parvenus), it no longer exercises the dictatorship of the proletariat, it is on top of the proletariat. On trade unions: It's very simple! One day I received official forms with an order to fill them in. I get forms all the time – and throw them in the wastepaper basket. As for new forms, the same: they get the same treatment. So, I received the same forms a third time, and with a final warning: if I did not return them properly filled in, my *payok* and that of my family would be stopped. The *payok* is the monthly food ration which the state provides for us. I would do anything not to lose that. I filled in the forms and sent them off. At the end of the month dues are deducted from my salary, and there you are, I have joined up! Every month, the same dues – that's the only contact I have with my trade union.

As for Lenin, (whom he disliked), and other burgeoning institutions of the regime – his comments poured out, with his customary candour, sweeping away every illusion. But I couldn't understand the contradiction between what he said, and what he wrote, in the revolutionary press in the West. At that point I did not understand things entirely, and being at the time unable to brusquely reject my friendship and admiration, I visited him once again and then we went off to Moscow.

[…] One day it was suggested that we should visit the colony of Bolchavo, situated fifty *versts* [30 miles] from Moscow. We were to spend two days there. I went off with Andre Nin[‡] and

† Hilario Arlandis, a CNT member, later a communist.
‡ A CNT member, later a dissident communist.

Arlandis. [...] Some 500 children ... enchanted us with games, conviviality, singing, and rhythmic steps. I asked two questions ...

'How are these children chosen to join the colony?' The female director replied: 'They are the children of party members, of state administrators, or of officers in the Red Army.' Next, since nothing had been said about professional teaching, and since no workshop were being shown to us, I asked: 'What professional [or trade] training do you give these children and from what age?' 'These children are destined to be state administrators; so they are given no manual instruction.'

It was a revelation. What was being prepared in the Bolchavo colony, and in other more or less similar establishments, organised under guidance from Lunacharsky, Minister of Public Education (and with the excellent teacher-training that Russia had known before the revolution), was not a free and egalitarian socialism for a free people but a cast of administrators, locating themselves above [ordinary] society.§

I returned to Moscow, and went to see Alexander Berkman and Emma Goldman, the two great anarchist agitators expelled from their home country by the US government because of their work in favour of the Russian revolution. I found them disheartened, reduced to inactivity, in complete disagreement

§ Vilkens had come to similar conclusion on the role of education in the new state. On the role of the new communist university system he concluded: 'It isn't hard to see that the goal of these institutions is one of preparing a class of bureaucrats who will monopolise every manifestation of political and economic life, and this will indefinitely reduce and obstruct any possibility of returning to direct participation by the worker and peasant masses. In this way, a fourth class, which has taken power and enjoys a privileged situation, high above the masses is growing and ceaselessly renewing itself; it will not – as a class – entertain committing suicide, saying one day to the people: "Well, we have organised everything, both material and spiritual life, we think the time has come to withdraw, to return into the masses from which we emerged." Affirming that the Communist state is marching on towards the disappearance of the state, towards Libertarian Communism – is farce and self-delusion; whoever says as much is lying, and whoever believes it is an imbecile.' *Le Libertaire*, 29 July 1921.

with the Bolshevik's conduct and politics. They talked of the recent pitiless crushing of the Kronstadt uprising, comparing it with the Paris Commune; of the suffocation by the police and bureaucracy of the soviets and trade unions of political repression that systematically eliminated everyone who would not accept the yoke of the new masters. They had been charged with facilitating the organisation of the Museum of the Revolution in Petrograd, but they had had to give up the project in the face of the impossibility of carrying through any serious or impartial work. (For the Bolsheviks, the only genuine revolutionaries were themselves.)

Neither did they want to be accomplices of the totalitarianism that was becoming stronger by the day. Thousands of revolutionaries were back in the prisons they had left when the Tsarist regime fell. Our movement was fragmented and was condemned little by little to illegality. In the Communist Party congress, Lenin repeated time and time again: 'We made mistakes', but said Emma Goldman, he neither tolerated others who said the same, nor did he begin to stop making mistakes.

I listened to their criticism with some disquiet, resolved to be quite impartial, ready to contradict my comrades, if need be. Because, for me, builders were ahead of destroyers. It wasn't enough to fight against the errors of others, their failings, or even crimes. I wanted to know how one might do better than them, so without equivocation I asked, 'What is the programme that you would have in opposition to that of the Bolsheviks?' Alexander Berkman replied, 'I'm in the process of drafting it', as he typed something in Russian.

They – mostly men – came from France, Germany, Italy, Switzerland, Canada, North and South America, Denmark, Sweden; so many because the congress of the Communist International was due to meet before the congress of the (trade) Union International. Soon I saw my friend Victor Serge among them – conversing, talking, smiling, chatting – always admirably convincing.

Again, hearing him talk, I was amazed. He was saying exactly the opposite of what he had told us in Petrograd. He repeated, more or less, every argument that had addressed in his articles in the revolutionary press in the West.[8] It is true he was with communists and he had to be on his guard. When some of the things he said shocked some delegates – he expressed his agreement with them – but then, through some clever turn, having said he was hurt by the effects on the victims, he demonstrated that these victims were in the wrong and had acted foolishly.

So, for example, he said it was inevitable that machine guns had to fire on people who doggedly climbed up on the roofs of railway wagons leaving Petrograd (because that was the only way they could get to see their families in the countryside) – and since then the practice of travelling without tickets or permits had stopped. It had been necessary, to bleed and strangle the uprising by the most clear-sighted popular revolutionaries in the Kronstadt insurrection, because, even if that insurrection was justified, it had been utilised by the counter-revolution. Makhno, the revolutionary anarchist who had struggled against the Bolsheviks in the Ukraine, was doubtless sincere, but any toleration of separatist currents was impossible, because it would have endangered the broader whole.

Victor Serge agreed with those delegates who wished to preserve the independence of the [workplace] union movement, he supported communist delegates who would not agree to subordinate themselves to the wishes of their Russian comrades, and he was pleased to see that Boris Souvarine¶ knew how to manoeuvre sensibly behind the scenes. He noted that two leaders of the Workers' Opposition[9] in the Russian Communist Party, Shlyapnikov and Alexandra Kollontai, would also have things to say.

Speaking before our entire delegation, gathered together to converse with him in one of the rooms of the *Lux* hotel, he spoke as a Bolshevik who understood workplace unionism, and

¶ Later a dissident communist, author of *Stalin: A critical survey of Bolshevism*, London: Secker & Warburg, 1939.

he sought to demonstrate the inadequacies of the movements that we represented and so justified the dictatorship of the Communist Party, saying:

We are still obliged to enforce a dictatorship. If you use force to eliminate the bourgeoisie, you are exerting a dictatorship against the bourgeoisie. Moreover, if one has to designate someone for a responsible position, then you are forced to say: 'such and such a person is not up to it, but another person, one like that, will do'. Or, if you say Peter is not right for the project that he is managing, and you give the job to James (someone better qualified), despite Peter being unhappy, then that too is dictatorship.

He slipped in through the cracks, inserting the tactics and principles of the party he served. He juggled arguments, cleverly using false analogies and easy sophistries, so that he could destroy [general] principles.

He spoke always of Russian anarchists and revolutionary syndicalists as being his friends, he even declared to certain French anarchists that he was still an individualist.[10] For a non-communist audience, such things inspired confidence. But, he added, these friends – although they might have undoubted good faith – committed errors and dangerous mistakes; and the Bolshevik regime whatever its failings was the only revolutionary option that remained; for the good of the Russian and world proletariat it should not be attacked.

In the four months of my stay in Moscow he made me sick at heart as I saw him practising these manoeuvres 'without conscious scruples', just as he did earlier when he defined himself as an individualist anarchist, at the time of the Bonnot gang.[11] As for revealing the truth – he relied on our past friendship that I should not open up; perhaps he thought I was too naïve and that I would not recognise the game he was playing. I discussed things with him at first,[12] then I gave him the cold shoulder. Later, when I returned to France I published an article in *Le Libertaire* in which I compared what he had told me and what he continued to write. He was too artful to accept any direct polemic; in *La Vie Ouvrière* he replied that he would not abase himself to reply to personal attacks, since the cause of the Revolution was above such petty things. I replied with further details citing names and dates. He remained silent on that occasion.

I had soon become convinced that my first informants were telling the truth. It was not just the anarchists who were suffered systematic repression, (some anarchists had a solely negative hostility which might have provoked the treatment they received), but every party, and every other tendency. The Left Socialist Revolutionaries who ruled with the Bolsheviks after the October revolution, had been outlawed. Their leader Maria Spiridonova, had been condemned for a terrorist attack when she was a young student. She was released from Tsarist prisons in 1917, only to find herself back in the same prisons in 1920. She would [eventually] die in prison.**

There was a long collaboration between the Bolsheviks and the Left Socialist Revolutionaries; their General Secretary Steinberg, was for a time Minister of Justice … After his experience of the Russian revolution Steinberg told me that he had concluded that one should prefer a regime that was much more authentically federalist and soviet rather than statist and governmental. As for Bolshevik politics, he summed up the new state of things as it existed in Russia in these words, words that I have never forgotten because they were so accurate and gave such a true description: 'What we [now] have is neither even a bourgeois republic, nor even a constitutional monarchy; no we have an absolute monarchy' […]

Revolutionary syndicalism had not existed in Russia; persecutions under Tsarism had prevented the creation of workers' syndicates like those of the French CGT. A few Russian revolutionaries, intellectuals rather, who had become syndicalists while they had been forced to spend some time abroad, could neither organise such a movement in this mad,

---

** Spiridonova was held intermittently in mental asylums, barracks and prisons between 1919 -1921; she was re-arrested in 1937 and executed in 1941.

statist regime nor promote its principles. The current situation was akin to that which had existed before 1914. But inside the Communist Party itself, a Workers' Opposition was agitating. We talked several times with its two best-known leaders, Shlyapnikov and Alexandra Kollontai (Kollontai seemed the more intelligent in my view). I remember clearly what Kollontai told us: [...]

At the congress in March of that year [1921], which took place immediately after the crushing of the workers' and sailors' insurrection in Kronstadt, by Trotsky, she distributed a pamphlet; we were able to acquire this clandestine text. In it she gave a magisterial refutation – from the viewpoint of pure doctrine – of Lenin and Trotsky (the latter, always gallant, treated her as a courtesan, as also he had treated Maria Spiridonova as hysterical) – and mocked Bukharin royally.

So, she set out the theses of the Workers' Opposition of the Communist Party with rigorous logic, a logic which, from the Marxist viewpoint, has not ceased to be valid. Marxism, she said, is based on historical materialism. The latter lent economic factors primacy over politics; also, because, in the chain of facts, one must accept dialectical reality. If such was the case, it was therefore logical that in a society established on Marxist principles, organisations representing purely economic realities, in the shape of the syndicates of workers, should be placed above a political organism, the state. Therefore, [thought Kollontai and Shlyapnikov] we demand for workers' syndicates the freedom to organise and make initiatives for themselves, and have an increasing role in the economic direction of socialist Russia.

The pamphlet was banned and confiscated,[††] and Lenin proposed a resolution, which was naturally voted through almost unanimously, in which the theses of the Workers' Opposition were likened to 'petty bourgeois and anarchist deviations'. It

---

[††] 5,000 copies of the pamphlet were printed, but to confuse international opinion the cover said 500,000 copies had been printed. Kollontai denounced these facts at the congress in March 1921, but to no effect.

declared that 'an inflexible and systematic struggle' was needed against these deviations.

The Workers' Opposition was muzzled by members of the Communist Party themselves, and in this way, there was inaugurated the repression which was later known within the party and which led on towards the Moscow trials.‡‡ I was able to speak twice to Alexandra Kollontai in the corridors of the rooms where the congress was taking place. 'We could do nothing', she said, 'we are condemned to absolute silence. Impossible to hold a lecture or the smallest little meeting, or to publish the smallest little journal. When we wanted to meet to exchange ideas or impressions, we did so with just four or five of us there, and having tea – to cover appearances.'

She told me again that she would not accept [the task of] promoting the majority's theses, and, she was able to speak in public less and less. From time to time she was ordered to travel to one town or another to defend positions that she rejected, because the party's iron discipline would not allow her to defend what she thought was right. 'But, I didn't go, I refused', she said resolutely. At this moment, Trotsky, in disagreement with Lenin, agreed to submit and promote things he did not believe. Indeed, it was this submission to Bolshevik discipline that made possible his defeat by Stalin.

[...] It was during a spell of a week in Petrograd (I had returned there to research a certain number of questions; I had some problems getting permission to travel, even though I was a delegate). One morning I arrived with a couple of comrades who worked at the Museum of the Revolution. I found them very upset.

'Did you hear the gunfire last night?' they asked.

'I heard nothing. It didn't get to me.'

'The whole of Petrograd is talking of it. Twenty people were shot: engineers, poets, writers, the intellectual flower of Petrograd. They were accused of speculation, of plotting against

---

‡‡ Of the late 1930s – in these many Old Bolsheviks were convicted and subsequently executed.

the regime. We knew many of them, and can assert that it was an abominable lie. The *Izvestía* newspaper, which had just arrived from Moscow, had already announced the executions, it listed the victims and described the crimes which served as a pretext for their condemnation.'

Counter-revolutionary plots and speculation – these two accusations had become classic pretexts. In their name, and without any control, the Cheka arrested, deported, judged, and assassinated. Nothing could stop them from their ongoing sequence of extermination.[13]

Leval asked to work in a Russian factory after the congress but permission was refused by Lozovoski. After leaving Russia Leval defended the creation of the independent syndicalist international that was organised in Berlin in late December 1921, and opposed participation in the 'Red' Labour Union International and the Communist International.[14]

NOTES

1   From: Xavier P Anlagua, 'La Visió de Gaston Leval de la Rússia Sovietica el 1921', *Recerques*, No. 3, Barcelona: Ariel, 1974, pp. 199-224. http://www.raco.cat/index.php/Recerques/article/viewFile/137507/241298 Gaston Leval's texts 'Esenanzas de Rusia', were published in *Redención*, (Alcoy) beginning in No. 70, 22 June 1922. (Available online: http://www.cedall.org).

2   Leval said that when he was appointed to balance the five-person CNT delegation sent to Russia, he was a sceptical anarchist. An article in the Argentinean journal *La Protesta*, 27 March 1922, said the delegation acted as one – except for Leval. Another article in that issue commented that the four communist delegates were promoting personal opinions at variance with the CNT generally. Llado concluded that the other delegates were radical Social-Democrats rather than libertarians. They were working to have the CNT absorbed and subordinated to orders from Moscow. Bruno Llado, 'El Congreso Internacional Sindical Rojo de Moscú. La actitud de la delegación de la C.N.T. de España.', *La Protesta* (Suplemento), No. 12, 27 March 1922. http://www.antorcha.net/index/hemeroteca/periodico_protesta/1922/1922.html

3   Leval portrayed Trotsky as an autocrat, unwilling to be questioned and accustomed to giving orders. *Redención*, No. 84 and 85, 19 and 26 October 1922.
4   *Redención*, No. 96, 11 January 1923.
5   Leval like Serge was a French speaker, both had spent war years in Spain.
6   Rirette Maîtrejean, (in *Souvenirs d'anarchie*, Quimperlé: La Digitale, 2005, pp. 94-95) suggests that Serge was courageous and wanted only to travel on to Russia. Luc Nemeth wrote that Serge wanted to 'serve' with Russians in France because he expected them to be repatriated to Russia. Serge was arrested, imprisoned and was only freed in January 1919. (Ibid, pp. 103-105).
7   See Victor Serge, 'The anarchists and the experience of the Russian revolution' in: *Revolution in Danger*, London: Redwords, 1997, and *Memoirs of a Revolutionary*, New York Review of Books, 2012. Serge also wrote about Bakunin, publicising his 'confession' to the Tsar. (See: https://www.marxists.org/reference/archive/bakunin/works/1851/confession.htm and https://www.marxists.org/francais/serge/works/1919/11/confession.htm) Wilkens's replies to Serge were published in *Le Libertaire* and in *La Antorcha*; a critique of Serge can be found here: http://anarchism.pageabode.com/anarcho/victor-serge-worst-anarchists
8   In the course of the congress of the Third International I asked Victor Serge-Kibalchich: What is your opinion of Bela-Kun? He replied: 'Evil, immoral, a nullity, cruel'. Those who exercise power are always the same. *Redención* (Alcoy), No. 70, 22 June 1922.
9   Documents on the Workers' Opposition can be found online: https://www.marxists.org/archive/kollonta/1921/workers-opposition/index.htm
10 Luc Nemeth, commented in 2003: 'What Serge often criticised thereafter wasn't anarchism [-in-general, but] only a particular form of anarchism, the one Serge had known in France at the time'; in Rirette Maîtrejean, *Souvenirs d'anarchie*, op. cit., p. 67.
11 See: Richard Parry: *The Bonnot Gang: The Story of the French Illegalists*, London: Rebel Press, 1987, pp. 33ff.
12 Leval quoted Serge and anarchist comrades as his source for a large part of his information when he published an initial list of 66 Anarchist prisoners. *Redención*, No. 73, 13 July 1922.
13 A further selection from this text, 'Anarchists behind bars' is included in Daniel Guerin, *No Gods, No Masters*, Vol. 2, Edinburgh: AK Press, 2005, pp. 593ff.
14 'La derrota de la sindical roja. Carta de Gastón Leval', *La Protesta* (Suplemento), No. 13, 3 April 1922.

The Crushing of the Russian Revolution
Emma Goldman[1]

Emma Goldman noted Lenin did admit past errors and did change policy. But each new policy became the new, final word of Marxism. As for critics – those who argued for policies that Lenin had advocated in the past, or those might argue for policies he had not yet sanctioned – they were enemies, to be classified as counter-revolutionaries, speculators or bandits.[2] Truth was distorted.

Emma Goldman spent some time in London. 'The Labour leaders were callous. In the words of a British Socialist, "It would spell political disaster to my party to declare to its constituents that the Bolsheviks had slain the Revolution"' The Independent Labour Party did not approve all the methods of the dictatorship but could not afford to campaign against it. She tried to explain that there she worked for other choices – beyond Bolshevism and Tsarism – but she had a hard time doing so. Her truths were little appreciated at this time.[3] Emma Goldman received support from *Freedom* but some other libertarians – notably Guy Aldred – took some time to appreciate what had developed in Russia.

Revolution

How did such a thing happen? Very simply. The Russian people, who alone had made the revolution and who were determined to defend it at all costs against the interventionists, were too busy on the numerous fronts to pay any attention to the enemy of revolution within. And while the workers and peasants of Russia were laying down their lives so heroically, this inner enemy rose to ever greater powers. Slowly but surely the Bolsheviks were building up a centralised State, which destroyed the Soviets and crushed the revolution, a State that can now easily compare, in regard to bureaucracy and despotism, with any of the great Powers of the world.

From my study and observation of two years I am certain that the Russian people, if not continuously threatened from without, would have soon realised the danger from within and would have known how to meet that danger, as they had the Kolchaks, Denikins,* and the rest of them. Free from imperialist counter-revolutionary attacks, the people would have soon become aware of the true tendencies of the Communist State, its utter inefficiency and inability to reconstruct ruined Russia.

The masses themselves would have then begun to infuse new life into the paralysed social energies of the country. Would not the people have erred and blundered, even as the Bolsheviks have? No doubt they would. But they would have, at the same time, learned to depend upon their own initiative and strength — which alone could have saved the revolution.

It is entirely due to the criminal stupidity of some of the ex-revolutionists who clamoured for intervention, and to the imperialists who financed and backed intervention, that the Russian Revolution, the greatest event of centuries, has been lost. To them it is also due that the Bolsheviks, wrapped in the cloak of persecution, can continue to pose as the holy symbol of the Social Revolution.

I mean to expose this fatal delusion. Not because I have lost faith in the revolution, but because I am convinced that coming revolutions are doomed to failure should what Lenin himself called military Communism be imposed on the world. Not because I have made peace with government do I intend to show what the Bolshevik regime has done to the Russian Revolution.

* 'White' – counter-revolutionary – Generals.

Rather is it because the experience of Russia, more than any theories, has demonstrated that all government, whatever its form or pretences, is a dead weight that paralyses the free spirit and activities of the masses.

I owe this to the revolution, nailed to the Bolshevik cross, to the martyred Russian people, and to the deluded of the world. I mean to pay my debt in full, regardless both of the misappropriation of my words by the reactionaries and of vilification by blinded radicals.

The Forces that Crushed the Revolution

The Russian Revolution – as a radical social and economic change – meant to overthrow capitalism and establish Communism must be declared a failure. In estimating the various factors that crushed the revolution, it is not enough to point out the role played by the counter-revolutionary elements. To be sure, their crimes are heinous enough to condemn them unto all eternity. These Russian 'patriots' – monarchists, Cadets (Constitutional Democrats), Right Socialist-Revolutionists, etc. – filled the world with their clamour for intervention. What was it to them that millions of their countrymen and thousands of innocent victims from all lands were slaughtered in the unholy war against Russia?

They lived in perfect safety and security; neither the bullets of the Cheka[†] nor the devastating hand of hunger and typhus could reach them. They could afford to play the game of patriotism. But, then, all this is sufficiently known to require no further elucidation. What is not known is that the Russian and Allied interventionists were not the only actors in the great social drama which ended in the death of the Russian Revolution. The other actors are the Bolsheviks themselves. It is of their role that I shall speak now.

Perhaps the Russian Revolution was doomed at its birth. Coming as it did upon the heels of four years of war, which

[†] The Extraordinary Commission to Fight Counter-Revolution and Sabotage, named from its initials in Russian. State security police.

had drained Russia of her best manhood, sapped her blood, and devastated her land, the revolution may not have had the strength to withstand the mad onslaught of the rest of the world. The Bolsheviks claim that the Russian people, though heroic enough for great outbursts, lack the perseverance necessary for the slow, painful, every-day exigencies of a revolutionary period. I do not admit the truth of it.

But, granted that this contention is well founded, I yet insist that it was not so much the attacks from without as the senseless and cruel methods within Russia that have killed the revolution and placed the yoke of despotism upon the people's neck. The Marxist policies of the Bolsheviks, the tactics first extolled as indispensable to the life of the revolution only to be discarded as harmful after they had wrought misery, distrust, and antagonism, were the factors that slowly undermined the faith of the people in the revolution.

If there ever was doubt as to what constitutes the greatest danger to a revolution – outside attacks or the paralysed interest of the people within – the Russian experience should dispel that doubt completely. The counter-revolutionists, backed by Allied money, men, and munitions, failed utterly; not so much by the heroism of the Red Army as by the revolutionary enthusiasm of the people themselves, who fought back every attack. Yet the Russian Revolution has died an agonised death. How, then, explain that phenomenon?

The main causes are not far to seek. If a revolution is to survive in the face of opposition and obstacles, it is of the utmost importance that the light of the revolution be held high before the people; that they should, at all times, be close to the living, throbbing pulse of the revolution. In other words, it is necessary that the masses should continuously feel that the revolution is of their own making, that they are actively participating in the difficult task of building a new life.

For a brief period after the October Revolution the workers, peasants, soldiers, and sailors were indeed the masters of their revolutionary fate. But soon the invisible iron hand began to manipulate the revolution, to separate it from the people, and to make it subservient to its own ends – the iron hand of the Communist State.

The Bolsheviks are the Jesuit order in the Marxist Church. Not that they are insincere as men, or that their intentions are evil. It is their Marxism that has determined their policies and methods. The very means they have employed have destroyed the realisation of their end. Communism, Socialism, equality, freedom – everything for which the Russian masses have endured such martyrdom – have become discredited and besmirched by their tactics, by their Jesuit motto that the end justifies all means.

Cynicism and coarseness have taken the place of the idealist aspirations that characterised the October Revolution. All inspiration has been paralysed; popular interest is dead; indifference and apathy are dominant. Not intervention nor the blockade – on the contrary, it was the internal policies of the Bolshevik State that alienated the Russian people from the revolution and filled them with hatred of everything emanating from it.

'What is the use of changing?' now say the people; 'all rulers are alike – the poor must always suffer.' It is this fatalism, coupled with submission of centuries, which has helped the Bolsheviks in their dominion over Russia. Have the Bolsheviks learned from experience that the end does not justify all means?

To be sure, Lenin often repents. At every All-Russian Communist conclave, he comes forth with his *mea culpa*, 'I have sinned.' A young Communist once said to me: 'It would not surprise me if Lenin should, someday, declare that the October Revolution was a mistake.' Indeed, Lenin does admit his mistakes; but that does by no means prevent him from continuing the same mistaken policies. Every new experiment is proclaimed by Lenin and his zealots as the height of scientific and revolutionary wisdom. Woe be to those who dare question the justice or efficacy of the new measure! They are branded as counter-revolutionists, speculators, and bandits.

But presently Lenin again repents, and then begins to deride his flock as fools for having believed that the experiment was at all possible. After deluding Russia and the world for four years by his avowal that Communism is in the making in Russia, Lenin at the last Congress of the All-Russian Soviets covered his comrades with ridicule for their naïveté in believing that Communism is realisable in Russia now. Yet the prison doors are still closed upon those who mildly suggested the same thing three years ago.

It would be interesting to trace the various methods employed by the Bolsheviks to achieve their ends – methods forced upon the people as the sum-total of all wisdom and which resulted in the undoing of the revolution. The scope of an article does not allow a detailed analysis of everything the Bolshevik State has done. I shall here refer only to the most important methods and phases.

The Brest-Litovsk peace‡ marked the beginning of all subsequent evils. It was a deliberate denial of all that the Bolsheviks had proclaimed to the world – peace without indemnities, self-determination of all oppressed peoples, no secret diplomacy. Yet the Bolsheviks made peace with German imperialism over the heads of the German people. The price of that peace was the betrayal of Latvia, Finland, the Ukraine, and Byelorussia [Belarus].

The result – several years of civil war, the disruption of the revolutionary forces, when unity was so vital to the defence of the revolution, and the beginning of Red terror which is continuing to this day. The peasantry of the Ukraine and of Byelorussia knew how to drive back the German invader, but it has neither forgotten nor forgiven the treachery of the Bolsheviks. The continuous presence of a million troops in the Ukraine to 'liquidate the bandits' bears witness to the love of the Ukrainian peasants for the Communist State. The ratification

---

‡ March 1918, treaty between German and its allies and the Soviet Russian state.

of the Brest peace, which Trotsky refused to sign, which Radek[§] – then in a German prison – declared as the bankruptcy of the revolution, while Joffe[¶] signed it 'with closed eyes,' as he said, was the signal for long open and secret resistance of the peasants to the Bolshevik State.

The peasants, who were at one with the workers till the Brest betrayal, turned with hatred and antagonism from the Bolsheviks, who claimed to represent the peasants and the workers. Lenin demanded the ratification as a breathing spell for the revolution. It was one of his many blunders, but the most costly one. It strangled the revolution.

Forcible Food Collection

The *Razvyorstka*, the method of forcible food collection, soon followed upon the heels of the Brest peace. The Bolsheviks will have it that they were compelled to resort to the *Razvyorstka* because of the refusal of the peasants to feed the city. This is only partly true. The peasants did indeed refuse to turn over their products to the Government agents. They demanded the right to deal with the workers directly, but it was denied them. The inefficiency of the Bolshevik regime and the corruption of their bureaucracy contributed much to the dissatisfaction of the rural population. The manufactures promised to the peasants in exchange for their produce seldom reached them, or, when actually received, proved to be damaged goods, short of measure, and so forth.

In Kharkov, I saw the demonstration of the inefficiency of the centralised bureaucratic machine. In a large factory warehouse, there lay huge stacks of agricultural machinery. Moscow had ordered them made 'within two weeks, in pain of punishment for sabotage.' They were made, and six months already had passed without the 'central authorities' making any effort to distribute the machines to the peasantry, which kept clamouring for them in their great need. It was one of the countless examples of the

[§] K B Radek, journalist, Bolshevik leader, active in the Comintern.
[¶] A A Joffe, Bolshevik, an associate of Trotsky.

manner in which the Moscow system 'worked,' or, rather, did not work.

Is it to be wondered at that the peasants lost all faith in the ability of the Bolshevik State to manage things properly? When the Bolsheviks saw that the peasant was not to be coaxed or cajoled into confidence, they devised the *Razvyorstka*. A more effective method for antagonising and embittering the peasantry could not have been invented. It became the dreaded terror of the agrarian population. It robbed them of everything. Only the future will be able to give an adequate picture of the terrible consequences of that insane measure, with its great sacrifice of life and devastation.

Unbelievable as it may seem, it is a fact well known in Russia that the *Razvyorstka* system was partly responsible for the present famine. For the peasants were not only stripped of their last pood** of flour; often they were robbed of the seeds they had put by for their next planting. The drought is, of course, the main cause of the harrowing conditions in the Volga districts. But it is nevertheless true that if the peasants had been able to plant at the proper time, and freely, at least certain areas would have been in a position to help lessen the famine on the Volga. The punitive expeditions, following upon a village's resistance to the Government's food collectors, and always in charge of Communists, would attack the place by force of arms and often literally destroy it. In vain the peasants protested to their local authorities, and finally to Moscow. No redress was to be found. A significant anecdote is current in Russia which throws light upon the peasants' view of the Bolshevik method of food 'collection.'

A peasant committee is received by Lenin.

'Well, de-dushka, little grandfather,' says Lenin to the oldest peasant, 'you should be satisfied now; you have the land, the cattle, the fowls; you have everything.'

'Yes, God be blessed,' replies the peasant; 'yes, little father, the land is mine, but you get the bread; the cow is mine, but

** A weight of approximately 16.4 kilogrammes.

yours the milk; the chicken mine, but yours the eggs. The Lord be blessed, little father!'

The peasants, thus robbed and duped, turned against the Communists. The *Razvyorstka*, the punitive expeditions, the brutal methods and injustices, resulted in producing a strong counter-revolutionary feeling in the country. Some writers on Russia have taken the Government's interpretation of the antagonism of the peasants.

Thus, Mr. Bertrand Russell, by far the most sincere and honest critic of Russia, states in *The Practice and Theory of Bolshevism*: 'It must be said that the peasants' reasons for disliking the Bolsheviks are very inadequate.' It is evident that Mr. Russell did not see the effects of the *Razvyorstka*, or he would have received a different impression. The truth is, if the Russian peasant were not so phlegmatic and passive, the Bolshevik State would not have endured so long. As it is, their passive resistance has come near terminating the Bolshevik regime. This realisation it was – not the fact that the *Razvyorstka* was inhuman and counter-revolutionary – which forced Lenin to his new policy of taxation and free trade.

The Co-operatives

The co-operatives of Russia represented a great economic and cultural force in the life of the people. In 1918 they covered the country with a chain of 25,000 branches, with a membership of 9,000,000. Their invested capital at that time amounted to 15,000,000 roubles, while the business transacted the previous year exceeded 200,000,000. Of course, the co-operatives were not revolutionary organisations, but they were an indispensable medium between the country and the city.

Whatever counter-revolutionary elements there were in the co-operatives were on top and could have been eliminated without destroying the entire organisation. But to permit the co-operatives to function would have meant the lessening of the centralised power of the State. Hence the co-operatives had to be 'liquidated,' and a great factor for the reconstruction of Russia was utterly destroyed.

Now, after the co-operatives are no more and the men and women that have done such splendid work in that movement have wasted their lives in Bolshevik prisons, Lenin again says, 'mea culpa'. The co-operatives are now to be re-established, the corpse is to be revived. Shortly before the co-operatives were again legalised, Peter Kropotkin – then on his deathbed – expressed the wish that the six Dmitrov co-operators should be released. He had known them intimately as earnest and devoted workers.[4]

They had then already spent eighteen months in the Butyrka, the Moscow prison, because of their loyalty to their work. They were released only after Lenin had declared that the co-operatives must be resurrected. It is hardly probable that the co-operatives will ever attain to their former strength and importance within the Bolshevik State.

The Soviets

To call present Russia Soviet Russia or the Bolshevik regime a Soviet Government is preposterous. The Soviets had their inception in the Revolution of 1905, and again came into being after the February Revolution. They have about as much relation to the Bolshevik Government as the early Christians had to the Christian Church.

The Soviets of peasants, workers, soldiers, and sailors were the spontaneous expression of the liberated energies of the Russian people. They represented the needs of the masses made articulate after centuries of silence. Already in May, June, and July of 1917 the dynamic force of the Soviets urged the workers to seize the factories and the peasants to take the land. The Soviets spread with great rapidity over Russia, fanned the flames of the October Revolution, and continued to function for many months after that event. Some social politicians failed to grasp their significance. The latter simply swept over them. The same would have happened to the Bolsheviks had they attempted to stem the onrushing tide of this movement.

But Lenin is a shrewd and subtle Jesuit; he joined in the popular cry, 'All power to the Soviets!' When he and his fellow-Jesuits were firmly in the saddle, the breaking up of the Soviets began. To-day they are like everything else in Russia – a shadow with the substance utterly crushed.

The Soviets now voice only the decision of the Communist Party. No other political opinion has any chance to get a proper hearing. The election methods practised by the Communists would fill Tammany Hall with envy. On my arrival in Russia I was told by a leading Communist that 'Boss Murphy and Tammany Hall have nothing on us.' Naturally, I thought that the man was joking. Soon I convinced myself that he had told the truth.

Every known device is employed by the Bolsheviks to swell the Communist vote. If ordinary pleading fails, threats of losing the *payok*[††] and of arrest do the work. The voters know what to expect. It is therefore obvious why the Communists invariably poll a majority. Still, the Mensheviks, Left Social Revolutionists, and even Anarchists have their representatives elected now and then – which is no small feat in Bolshevik Russia.

Without a Press, deprived of free speech, and without the legal permission of propaganda in the shops, it is nothing short of a miracle that the opposing parties succeed in having some representation in the Soviets. But as far as opportunity of making themselves heard is concerned, they might as well not be there. The Communist chorus see to it that none but Communists are given a hearing.

In case of the Anarchists elected to the Soviets, the Government generally refuses to recognise their mandates or finds some pretext to send them to the Cheka. In 1920, I attended an election meeting held in one of the factory clubs in Moscow. It was the second time the Government had refused to seat the candidate of the workers – an Anarchist. Though the opposing

†† The payok was the official ration, it was steeply graded.

candidate of that district was Semashko, the Commissar of Health, the workers for the third time elected the Anarchist. In vain did Semashko stoop to abuse and misrepresentation; in vain did he shake his fist in the faces of the workers, calling anathema upon their heads.

The workers only laughed and jeered him and re-elected the Anarchist. A few months later the man was arrested on some pretext. He was released only after a prolonged hunger strike, and that only because the British Labour Mission was in Moscow at the time and the Bolsheviks were anxious to avoid a scandal. Before I left Moscow, 1 December 1921, three Anarchist members of the Moscow Soviet had been arrested. One was exiled from the capital; the other two, as I have learned since, have had a charge of 'banditry and underground activities', placed against them – a very serious charge, usually followed by shooting without hearing or trial. Those men had been outspoken in the Soviet. They had to be 'removed.'

One can easily see that neither the Moscow Soviet nor any other Soviet has any independent voice or function. Not even the ordinary Communist member has much freedom of speech there. In the Soviets, as well as in the entire Bolshevik Government, the 'dictatorship of the proletariat' is vested in the hands of a very small group – the inner circle which alone rules Russia and her people.

What was once an ideal, the free expression of the workers, peasants, and soldiers, has been turned into a farce, which the people no longer believe in or want.

Conscript Labour

Mobilisation of labour, in reality conscript labour, was heralded to the world as the greatest asset of Communism. 'All must labour now in Soviet Russia. No more parasites!' Though Lenin has never openly admitted that this method, like many other similar ones decreed to rebuild Russia, is a mistake, I am yet inclined to think that he realises that conscript labour has done absolutely nothing to increase the output of the workers.

What it did accomplish was to establish, while it existed, chattel slavery and to replace the bourgeois parasite by the machinery of Bolshevik parasitism. Its function was to drive the workers to toil, oversee them on the job, and have them arrested and occasionally even shot for deserting the job. As for the great majority of the workers, they went to the shops not to work but to rest, and secretly to make a few articles that their wives and children could take to the country and exchange for flour and potatoes. That, incidentally, kept them from starvation.

Apropos of the opportunities of bringing something from the country, a whole book could be written on that alone. With the prohibition of trading came the *zagryaditelny stryad*, the detachment of soldiers and Chekists at every station to confiscate everything brought by private persons to the city. The wretched people, after untold difficulties of obtaining a pass for travel, after days and weeks of exposure at the stations, after the ghastly trip in filthy, overcrowded cars, or on the roofs and platforms, would bring a pood of flour or potatoes, only to have it snatched from them by the *stryad*.

In most cases the confiscated stuff was divided by the defenders of the Communist State among themselves. The victims were fortunate indeed if they escaped further trouble. Often, they would be robbed of their precious pack and thrown into gaol for 'speculation.' The number of real speculators apprehended was insignificant in comparison with the mass of unfortunate humanity that filled the prisons of Russia for trying to keep from starving to death.

One thing must be said for the Bolsheviks – they do nothing by half. As soon as compulsory labour became a law, it was carried into effect with a vengeance. Men and women, young and old, thinly clad and in torn shoes, or with only rags on their feet, were indiscriminately driven into the cold and sleet to shovel snow or cut ice. Sometimes they were sent in groups to the forests to saw wood.

Pleurisy, pneumonia, and tuberculosis resulted. It was only then that the wiseacres in the Kremlin created a new department for the distribution of labour. This bureau decided upon the physical fitness of the workers, classified and distributed them according to their trade.

Under such enslaving and degrading conditions one need not be surprised that the people shirked the work, because they hated it and the way they were driven to it. They began to look upon the Communist State as the new leech that was sapping their life-blood. The workers of Petrograd, the most revolutionary, they who had borne the brunt of the long struggle, who had so heroically defended the city against Yudenitch,[‡‡] who starved and froze beyond belief –what wonder if even they came to loathe the false revolutionists and everything connected with them?

Not theirs is the fault – it is the cruel Bolshevik machine which undermined their ideals and faith. That machine has engendered a counter-revolutionary feeling which it will take long to overcome.

I shall never forget a certain scene – a meeting of the Petrograd Soviet. On that night, the fate of Kronstadt was to be decided. After long speeches by the leading Communists, several workers and sailors asked for the floor. A worker from the arsenal speaks. He faces the chair instead of the audience. His voice is tense with suppressed emotion, his eyes burn, his whole frame shakes. He addresses the Chairman of the Petrograd Soviet, Zinoviev.

'Three years and a half ago,' he says, 'you were denounced as a German spy, a traitor to the revolution, hounded and persecuted. We, the workers and sailors of Petrograd, saved you, and carried you to the seat you now occupy. We did that because we believed that you were expressive of the people. Since then you and your Government have gone away from us. Now you call us insulting names, dare to decry us as counter-revolutionists. You imprison and shoot us because we ask you to make good the promise you had given us in the October Revolution.'

[‡‡] A white General.

I do not know what became of the man. He may be in prison or dead for his daring. His cry fell on deaf ears. Yet it was the cry of an agonised spirit, the collective Russian spirit, that had aspired to and attained such heights during the Revolution and that is now fettered by the Bolshevik State.

The Cheka

The Cheka, the All-Russian Extraordinary Commission, unquestionably is the blackest measure of the Bolshevik regime. It was organised shortly after the Bolsheviks came to power for the purpose of coping with counter-revolution, sabotage, and speculation. Originally the Cheka was controlled by the Commissariat of the Interior, the Soviets, and the Central Committee of the Communist Party. Gradually it became the most powerful organisation in Russia. It was not merely a State within a State; it was a State over a State. The whole of Russia is covered to the remotest village with a net of Chekas.

Every department in the vast bureaucratic machine has its Extraordinary Commission, omnipotent over the life and death of the Russian people. It would require the master pen of a Dante to bring home to the world the inferno created by this organisation, the brutalising, disintegrating effect it has upon the Extraordinary Commissions themselves, the dread, distrust, hatred, suffering, and death it has wrought upon Russia.

The head of the All-Russian Extraordinary Commission is Dzerzhinsky. He, together with his fellow-members of its presidium, are "tried' Communists. In a public statement, Dzerzhinsky said: 'We are the representatives of organised terror.... We terrorise the enemies of the Soviet Government. ... We have the power to undertake raids, confiscate goods and capital, perform arrests, question, try, and condemn those we consider guilty, and to inflict the death penalty.'

In other words, the Cheka is spy, policeman, judge, gaoler, and executioner, all in one. It is the supreme power from which there is no redress, and only rarely an escape. It operates nearly always at night. The sudden flood of light in a district, the noise of madly speeding Cheka automobiles are signals for the alarm and dread of the community. The Cheka is at work again!

'Who are the unfortunates caught in the net this night? Whose turn will be next?'

The Cheka was organised to cope with counter-revolution, but for every real conspiracy it has unearthed it has created nine, either of an imaginary nature or of its own making. It must be borne in mind that the main asset of the Cheka are its provocateurs and informers. Like the scourge of typhus, they infest the very air of Russia. They shrink from no method, be it ever so base and cruel, to involve their victims and to penalise them as dangerous counter-revolutionists and speculators. In reality, however, the Cheka itself is a hotbed of counter-revolutionary plot and fabulous speculation.

Every Communist, by the discipline of his party, must at any time be ready to serve in the Cheka. But the majority of the Chekists are from the Tsar's 'Okhrana,'[§§] from the Black Hundreds, and from the former high officials of the army. They are adepts in the application of barbarous methods.

The Western world has been fed on glowing accounts of the people's tribunals in Russia — the courts presided over by workers and peasants. There are no such courts within the domain of the Cheka. Its proceedings are secret. The so-called hearings, when they take place at all, are a travesty of justice.

The 'culprit' is confronted by ready-made evidence; he has no witnesses, and is permitted no defence. When he is led away from the Chamber of Horrors, he does not even know whether he is acquitted or condemned. He is kept in maddening suspense until some night he is called out – never to return. The following morning a Chekist calls for his belongings, and the rest of the prisoners know that another cold-blooded murder has been added to the countless numbers.

And the relatives and friends of the unfortunates? They go on standing in line on the Lubianka, the street where the ghastly Cheka is quartered, for days and weeks anxiously waiting for

[§§] Secret police.

word from their own. At last they are told that the one they are looking for has been shot the previous night. In most cases the victim has been dead for a long time. Thus, insult is added to the tragedy and grief of the mourner.

Like the Okhrana of old, the Bolshevik Okhrana keeps its evil doings from the public. But the truth will out sometimes. There is already considerable printed data on the horrors within the walls of the Cheka – the brutal tortures, the graft, the widespread speculation. One need not go for information to the opponents of the Bolshevik regime. The Cheka itself occasionally furnishes much material. The weekly organ of the Cheka No. 3 contains an article on the necessity of torture. It is entitled 'Enough Sentimentality!' and says, among other things: 'In dealing with enemies of Soviet Russia, it is necessary to use methods of torture to press confessions out of them, and then despatch them to the other world.'

The reader need not think that the Cheka has progressed since 1918. Last summer, when the alleged plot of Professor Tagantsev was discovered in Petrograd, brutal beatings, torture by thirst, and such other eminently 'revolutionary' methods were employed. I have this information not from counter-revolutionists, but from a very sincere Communist who was one of the arrested, and who witnessed the results of Chekist methods.

A Communist among arrested counter-revolutionists? How did he get there? Very simply. When the Cheka throws out its net, it catches the innocent as well as the guilty; in fact, mostly the innocent. For how can sixty-eight persons be involved in a conspiracy without the whole city knowing it? Yet sixty-eight persons were shot last summer in Petrograd in connection with the Tagantsev 'plot.' And that is a small percentage of the innocent men, women, and even youths done to death in the cellars of the Cheka.

Time and again demands were made on the Government to check the power of this terrible organisation. Such an attempt was made in the fall of 1920. Immediately crime became rampant in Moscow, and 'conspiracies' multiplied. Naturally, the Cheka had to prove that it is indispensable to the Bolshevik State. Thereupon a testimonial of thanks was voted to Dzerzhinsky and published in the *Pravda*.

Zinoviev, at one of the sessions of the Petrograd Soviet, declared Dzerzhinsky 'a saint devoted to the revolution.' The history of the Dark Ages is full of such saints. How terrible that the Bolshevik regime must imitate the black past!

In this connection, it is interesting to recall the stand taken by the Bolsheviks in 1917, when the Provisional Government attempted to reinstate capital punishment for army deserters. At that time the Bolsheviks protested vehemently against such brutality. They pointed out how barbarous the death penalty is, and how degrading to mankind. After the October Revolution, at the Second All-Russian Congress of the Soviets, the Bolsheviks – together with the other revolutionary elements – voted to abolish capital punishment. Now *razstrels* [shootings] are the cherished method of the Cheka – methods presided over by a Communist saint and sanctioned by the Communist State.

What becomes of Marxism, which teaches that the Social Revolution is the birth of a new social life? Is there any indication of it in any of the Bolshevik principles and methods as applied in Russia? The Bolshevik State has proved itself a crushing conspiracy against the Russian Revolution.

The Persecution of Maria Spiridonova

Pre-revolutionary Russia stood unique in the world's history for the host of women she contributed to the revolutionary movement. Beginning with the Decembrists, whose wives followed them, nearly a century ago, into exile, down to the last hour of the Tsar's regime, Russian women participated in the most heroic activities and went to katorga, or death, with a smile upon their lips. Among the great number there stands out as one of the most remarkable figures Maria Spiridonova.

During 1905-1906 there was much unrest among the peasantry of Russia. In the province of Tambov, the peasants, exasperated by excessive taxation and the brutality of officials, rose against their oppressors and set fire to some estates. The Governor of Tambov, Luzhenovsky, known far and wide for his savagery, had whole villages flogged by the Cossacks. Half-naked, the peasants were forced to kneel for hours in the deep snow, while scores of them were stood up in rows and massacred. Maria Spiridonova was then a young girl, yet she was entrusted by her party, the Social-Revolutionists, with the task of avenging the barbarity practised upon the peasants – to kill Luzhenovsky.

It was a difficult task. Luzhenovsky was well guarded. With his Cossack punitive expeditionary force, he had for years travelled from village to village, terrorising the population and draining the peasants of their last provisions to feed the war with Japan. But the difficulties did not dismay Spiridonova. Disguised as a peasant woman, she became the shadow of Luzhenovsky. She haunted the railway stations and country roads 'in search,' as she explained, 'of her missing soldier husband.'

In spite of imminent danger, privation, and cold, she kept her long, vigilant watch for the Governor, till at last the looked-for opportunity arrived. As the train bearing Luzhenovsky pulled up at the station where Spiridonova had been waiting so patiently and he stepped on the platform, surrounded by his officers. Spiridonova broke through the cordon of guards and shot him to death.

The Russian Tsars were never partial in their treatment of women politicals, they were equally relentless toward both men and women. But in the case of Spiridonova the henchmen of Tsar Nicholas surpassed even the methods of Ivan the Terrible. She was subjected to unspeakable barbarities. Dragged to the waiting-room of the station, she was beaten into insensibility, her clothes torn from her body, and then turned over to her drunken guards.

These amused themselves by burning her naked body with lighted cigarettes, kicking her about the room, and finally outraging her. For weeks, she hovered between life and death, and then the death sentence was imposed on her. The news of the torture of Spiridonova aroused the whole world to protest, which saved her from the scaffold. She was sent to Siberia for life, where – as Gershuni afterwards related – she arrived 'a mere bundle of raw flesh.' In prison her comrades tenderly nursed her back to recovery. But the result of her ghastly experience remained with her – tuberculosis, a crippled hand, and the loss of the sight of one eye. But though physically marred and broken, her spirit continued aflame.

The February revolution opened the living grave for all Russian politicals, among them also Maria Spiridonova. Who can describe her exultation when she received the news of liberty? Yet she would not leave the prison until assured that all politicals were to be set free. Amid great acclamations of the people, Maria Spiridonova returned to Russia. But not to live in the Winter Palace, not to be feted, not to rest upon her laurels. She came back to throw herself into the mounting sea of the released energies of the masses, of the peasantry especially, who so revered and trusted her. She became Chairman of the Executive Committee of the All-Russian Soviet of Peasant Representatives.

As such she inspired, organised, and directed the newly awakened spirit and activities of the peasants. Unlike some of the old revolutionists who had for years fertilised the revolutionary soil with their tears and blood, and yet could not grasp the trend of the new time, Maria Spiridonova quickly realised that the February revolution was but the prelude to a greater and more profound change.

When the October revolution, like a mighty avalanche, overwhelmed many of the old revolutionary guard, Spiridonova remained firm in her revolutionary faith and at the side of the people in the hour of their greatest need. Day and night, she worked, always at the service of her beloved peasants.

She was the soul of the Department of Agriculture, and elaborated a plan for the socialisation of the land, one of the most vital problems of Russia at that time. How her frail body and weakened lungs withstood the tremendous strain is indeed a miracle. Only her great will power and marvellous devotion could successfully sustain her during that most difficult and intense period.

Already, early in 1918, Maria Spiridonova became aware that the revolution might be in greater danger from some of its friends than from its enemies. The Bolsheviks, swept into power by their revolutionary slogans borrowed partly from Anarchists and partly from the Social-Revolutionists, soon entered upon a different path. The first step in that direction was the Brest-Litovsk peace.

Lenin insisted on the ratification of that 'peace' only 'to gain a breathing spell for the revolution.' Maria Spiridonova, as well as many other revolutionists of different schools, to whom the revolution was not a mere laboratory for political experiments, determinedly fought the ratification. They contended that such a peace involved the betrayal of the Ukraine, then enthusiastically and victoriously driving the German invaders from Southern Russia; that it meant the exclusive domination of the Russian people by the Bolshevik Party and the suppression of all other political movements, with consequent bitter civil war; in short, the 'breathing spell' of Lenin would prove the complete debacle of the revolution.

At that time, Trotsky and many other Communists were opposed to the Brest-Litovsk peace. They, too, saw the danger ahead. But they were soon whipped into acceptance by the iron discipline of the party. Lenin carried the day, and the Calvary of the Russian Revolution began.

While in America, I had heard many conflicting stories about the fate of Maria Spiridonova in Soviet Russia. On my arrival, there I immediately made enquiries concerning her. I was informed by responsible Communists that she had suffered a nervous breakdown, become acutely hysterical, and was therefore placed in a sanatorium 'for her own good, and receiving the best of care.'

It was not till July 1920, that I had the opportunity to meet her. I found her living in Moscow, illegally, in a small room, again in the disguise of a peasant woman she used to assume in the days of the Tsar. She had escaped from the 'sanatorium and the best of care,' which had proved to be a Bolshevik prison. I found no trace of hysteria in Maria Spiridonova. What I did find was one of the most poised, self-controlled, and calm persons I had met in Russia till then.

During two days, I was held rapt by her account of the Russian Revolution; how the people had risen to sublime heights of great hopes and possibilities, and had then been hurled to the depths of misery and despair by the Communist State machine. It was a story of remarkable clarity and force of conviction.

It was then I learned that she had been imprisoned twice by the Bolsheviks. The first time was after the killing of Mirbach [the German Ambassador], when the Bolsheviks had closed the Fifth Congress of the Soviets and arrested the whole Left Social-Revolutionist faction led by Spiridonova. Released after five months, she was again arrested at the end of January, 1919, and incarcerated in a 'sanatorium' — not because of hysteria or mental breakdown, but because she could not be cajoled or bribed into accepting the so-called Proletarian Dictatorship.

She had freely spoken to the people of the dangers to the revolution from the new policies of the Bolsheviks, and the people had heard her gladly. The Bolsheviks pretended to the world, Spiridonova explained, that the fierce persecution of the Left Social-Revolutionists following their execution of Mirbach was due to an alleged attempt by them to seize governmental power. She was emphatic in the denial — and her words are substantiated by a mass of documentary evidence — that her faction ever intended or attempted seizure of power from the Communists.

The Spiridonova faction regarded the Brest-Litovsk peace as the rankest betrayal of the revolution. They considered the presence of Mirbach in Soviet Russia as an insult and a menace of imperialism. They openly called for the death of Mirbach and for an uprising against German invasion. They saw the revolution in danger. They openly avowed their beliefs, but neither Spiridonova nor her comrades had any knowledge of or part in any plot to seize power.

After the killing of Mirbach, Spiridonova herself came to the session of the Fifth All-Russian Congress of Soviets for the purpose of reading the official declaration of her faction that explained the necessity and the justification of Mirbach's death. She and her comrades were fully prepared to take the consequences of that act. The Bolsheviks prevented the reading of that document by closing the Fifth Congress and arresting the entire peasant representation, with Maria Spiridonova at their head.

In September 1920, the Cheka was again busy proving its usefulness to the revolution by one of its periodic raids and discovery of plots. In the raid which took place in Moscow the hiding place of Maria Spiridonova was accidentally discovered. She was then sick with typhus, and could not be removed. The house was surrounded by a heavy guard, and no one from the outside admitted to her.

When the crisis was over, Spiridonova, though still very ill, was removed to the Ossobi Otdell (Secret Police Section) and placed in the prison hospital. So grave was her condition that another arrested Left Social-Revolutionist, a woman friend of Maria's Siberian days, was permitted to take care of her. Both were kept under strictest surveillance, without the possibility of communicating with their friends.

In June 1921, a letter was received from the prison, painting the dismal picture of her terrible life. The constant watch of the 'comrades,' Chekists, the solitary confinement, the deprivation of mental and physical food were slowly accomplishing what the tortures under the Tsar had failed to do. Spiridonova had developed scurvy – her limbs were swollen, teeth and hair falling out. Added to this was the hallucination that she was being pursued by the gendarmes of the Tsar and the Chekists of Lenin. At one time, she had attempted to starve herself to death. The Cheka threatened forcible feeding, but finally acceded to the demand of Spiridonova's two closest friends, Izmailovitch and Kamkov, themselves prisoners, to let them coax Maria into accepting nourishment.

During the two Congresses in Moscow, held in July 1921, the comrades of Spiridonova circulated a manifesto which had been sent by them to the Central Committee of the Communist Party and to the main representatives of the Government, calling attention to the condition of Maria Spiridonova and demanding her release for the purpose of adequate medical treatment and care. A prominent foreign woman delegate to the Third Congress of the Communist International was approached in the matter. Later she was reported as having seen Trotsky, who had said that Spiridonova was still too dangerous to be liberated. It was only after accounts of her condition had appeared in the European Socialist press that she was released, with the proviso that she is to return to prison on recovery. Her friends who are taking care of her are now facing the alternative of either letting Spiridonova die or see her back in 'the best of care' of the Cheka.

One thing only can save Maria Spiridonova – the opportunity to leave Russia. Her friends have made such a demand upon the Bolshevik Government, but so far in vain. In 1906 the protest of the civilised world saved the life of Spiridonova. It is indeed tragic that a similar protest is again needed in her behalf. Away from the watchful eye of the Cheka, from the woe and distress of tortured Russia, somewhere in the free, pure mountain air, Maria Spiridonova may again recover. She has suffered a hundred deaths. Will she be given back to life?

Since this article was written, the Russian Red Cross of Moscow requested Unschlicht, the Chairman of the Moscow Cheka, now renamed Political Okhrana, that Spiridonova be permitted to leave Russia. In reply, this faithful defender of the Bolshevik State is supposed to have said that the conditions in Europe would be harmful to Spiridonova's health, hence she could not be given the chance to go abroad. This excuse given by Unschlicht is very strange, in view of the fact that European conditions do not seem to have harmed the health of the Russian delegation in Genoa. Neither have they affected any of the numerous representatives of the Bolsheviks who swarm the capital cities of Europe. Why, then, should European conditions harm Maria Spiridonova?

The fact of the matter is Unschlicht's excuse is only one of the many brazen evasions the Bolsheviks always make whenever they want to get out of a difficult position. They not only do not care for the welfare of Spiridonova, but they have done everything to get rid of her, and would, no doubt, heave a sigh of relief if she would oblige them by going out of life altogether. Since she has been released on parole, not the Bolsheviks, but the Red Cross and Spiridonova's personal friends have ministered to her needs. Why, then, this sudden solicitude on the part of Unschlicht?

The truth of the matter is, Spiridonova has remained irreconcilable. In Russia, she is gagged; in Europe, her voice might be heard. Mr. Unschlicht knows that, the Kremlin knows that. Therefore, she is not permitted to leave. However, the workers of Europe must not be hoodwinked by the excuses given by Unschlicht. They must make a decided and persistent demand upon the Bolshevik Government for the release of Maria Spiridonova. It is the least the revolutionary workers can do for one who has fought so long and so heroically for the oppressed of Russia and of the rest of the world. Maria Spiridonova, whom neither the Tsar nor the Bolshevik Government could bribe, cajole, or subdue, has the right to ask the support of the revolutionary proletariat to help her out of the tender care and solicitude of the Unschlichts and their Government.

The Care of the Children

The vicious circle created by the Communist State, and which thwarts the most sincere endeavours, is nowhere so evil and apparent as in the Bolshevik activities in behalf of the child. For though much of the accounts of child life in Russia is mere legend, still it must be admitted that a great attempt had been made. Why has it failed?

I remember vividly the impression made upon me by one of the speakers at the second anniversary of the October Revolution, held in Madison Square Garden, in 1919. The man had just returned from Russia. He roused the audience to great enthusiasm by his description of the care and treatment of the children in Russia. My heart went out to the people of that country — the masses who had thrown off the yoke of ages and were now being 'led by the hand of a child.' It was so wonderful.

All through my voyage on the floating prison [ship], *The Buford*, the thought of the work done for children in Russia sustained and warmed my spirit. How full of promise was the future; how inspiring to become part of that splendid new life! But in Russia I realised that I had reckoned without the vicious circle – the Socialist State which has compressed every effort within its orbit.

It is true that the Bolsheviks have attempted their utmost in regard to the child and education. It is also true that if they have failed to minister to the needs of the children of Russia, the fault is much more that of the enemies of the Russian Revolution than theirs. Intervention and the blockade have fallen heaviest upon the frail shoulders of innocent children and the sick. But even under more favourable conditions the Bureaucratic Frankenstein monster of the Bolshevik State could not but frustrate the best intentions and paralyse the supreme effort made by the Communists in behalf of the child and education.

It was not until I had been in Russia several weeks that I had an opportunity to visit the first school, the best in Petrograd. It is called *pokazatelnaya shkola*, model school, literally 'show school.' I did not grasp its meaning until later. The school was situated in the Hotel de l'Europe, the place still retaining much of its former elegance, with spacious rooms, beautiful chandeliers, and luxurious furniture.

In the winter of 1920 the shortage of fuel was so great in Petrograd that the population all but perished. It was therefore necessary to crowd the children in as few rooms as possible. But they were clean, well kept, and comfortable. The children, averaging from six to thirteen years, looked healthy, well fed, and contented. The physician in charge conducted me through the place, including the kitchen, shining with lovely copper dishes, and explained everything in detail.

The school was used as a sort of receiving and distributing centre. Children were brought there from all part of Russia, from the provinces mostly. They came in vermin-eaten clothes, emaciated and ill. They were bathed, weighed, measured, fed up, and given general treatment. For a short period, they remained in the school receiving elementary instruction, and later they were sent to other boarding schools for children. What I saw impressed me tremendously. Here, indeed, was proof of the reports that had come to America about the great things done for children in Russia.

There was only one disturbing note in the beautiful picture. A chance remark of my hostess, the physician, disclosed that several children could not be seen because 'they were in isolation.' 'Some contagious disease?' I asked. 'No,' said the lady, 'but they are little thieves, so we must keep them away from the other children.' I was dumbfounded. I saw before me the schoolmaster Tolstoy as portrayed by Ernest Crosby. One of the children in his school had stolen something. The other children had denounced him as a thief and asked their teacher to punish him. Pupils and teacher agreed that a sign bearing the inscription 'Thief!' should be hung on the offender's neck.

While putting the string over the boy's head, Tolstoy was struck by the look in the child's eyes – a look of humiliation and dumb accusation. No, not the child was the offender. It was he, Tolstoy, and the other children – all of society – that could commit such a cruel thing, to brand the child a thief. Never again thereafter was a child punished in Tolstoy's school. Yet here in great, free, revolutionary Russia were children punished, kept isolated, branded thieves, and continuously spoken of as 'moral defectives.' I was disturbed, and puzzled. However, I would not let that obscure the beautiful picture I saw in the Hotel de l'Europe.

A little later I was visited by a woman I had known in America for many years. With her husband and young son, she had rushed to their native land shortly after the February Revolution. She had participated in the great October days, and since then she had been engaged in various work, but her main interest was in the care of children. At the time of her visit she was matron in an *internat*, a boarding school for girls. The woman related to me much about her work, the children, and spoke of the bitter struggle to procure the necessary things for her school. Her story was so utterly at variance with what I had seen at the Hotel de l'Europe that I could not credit it. Yet I knew my friend to be absolutely honest and trustworthy. It seemed inexplicable.

I asked my friend to remain for supper. We talked about people we both had known in America, about the October Revolution and its effect upon the oppressed, of the world, while I was peeling potatoes in my improvised kitchenette.

'Don't throw the peelings away,' my friend warned me.

'Why, what do you want with the peelings?' I asked.

'The children make potato cakes of them and are so glad to get them.'

'The children?' I wondered. 'How is that possible? Are they not getting the first rations?' I saw myself at the Hotel de l'Europe that the children were fed on milk, cocoa, rice, farina, white bread, chocolate, even meat.

My visitor smiled. 'Come to my school,' she said, 'and convince yourself.'

I went, not once but many times. There I saw the other side of the medal. Yet even then I would not be convinced so easily. There were sixty-five children in that school. Their food was scanty and of poor quality. Most of them were sustained by what their people or relatives sent from the country. They had little warm clothing, and the majority were without shoes. My friend had to waste much of her time and all her energy in the various departments of the Education Board.

It took her two weeks to get twenty wooden spoons for her sixty-five children. After a whole month of effort, of standing in line, waiting to be admitted to the high officials, she was given twenty-five pairs of snowshoes. It required much wisdom and great tact to divide these among the sixty-five children without causing envy, hatred, and quarrels among them. Each time I revisited that school I became more convinced that there was something wrong somewhere. How else explain the difference between the care the children received at the Hotel de l'Europe and those of the school on Kronverski Prospekt?

There the children were given the best of everything – food, clothing, rooms, concerts, dances – in fact, almost too much considering the general situation. Here the children had so little that they were constantly hungry, and what little they got had to be obtained with the greatest difficulty.

Soon I learned a few facts. There was not enough food or clothing in Russia for all the children. The Bolsheviks thought it necessary to have a few show schools in each city for the benefit of the foreign missions, delegations and reporters. The children were exhibited, paraded on every occasion, and written about. These schools received the cream of everything. What was left went to the other schools, which were of course in the majority.

Persons that visited the show schools only and judged of the care of children in Russia by them went away utterly ignorant of the true conditions of the mass of children under the Bolshevik regime.

Allied intervention and the blockade are chiefly responsible for the terrible poverty in Russia. Yet whatever there was of life's necessities for the children could have been distributed more equitably. The Bolshevik system itself involved discrimination and inequality in regard to the children, as it did in the treatment of the workers. For the latter, there were various categories of rations, officially planned and carried out.

For the children, the same situation obtained in practice, though more unofficially. In the first place, the system of 'show' schools itself was vicious, demoralising, and establishing special privileges. That in return involved pretence, sham, and deceit, which could not help having their effect upon teachers as well as children.

But most of all, it was the centralisation of the State and its resultant complex machinery of bureaucratic officialdom that made the best efforts of the Bolsheviks, in this as in other directions, futile and barren.

'Dead Souls'

A hundred years ago, Gogol startled his countrymen by his great work *Dead Souls*. It was a scathing arraignment of Russian feudalism and its parasitism. *Dead Souls* have come to life again in Russia. But there is no Gogol to pillory them. And if there were, he would have much less chance of a hearing in the Russia of to-day than the great Gogol had in his time.

Who are the modern dead souls? That will be best clarified by illustration. Every crèche, boarding school, reformatory — in fact, every institution where children and grown people live — is entitled to as many food and clothing rations as the number of its inmates. All institutions depend on the Central Distributing Department (in Petrograd, the Petrokommuna; in Moscow, the Moskommuna, etc.)[55] for their supplies. Numerous orders signed and countersigned by scores of chinovniks [officials] must be secured for everything needed by a given institution.

The chinovnik systematically delaying matters until they receive some bribe, it becomes necessary to get orders for more than the actual number of the population in the institution, so that some 'extras' may be left for bribes as well as for the hungry friends of the 'economic manager' of the institution in charge of the supplies.

For instance, the school of my friend had sixty-five children. All former matrons had added a number of fictitious names – 'dead souls' – to the actual total of the children in the schools. In return for the extra rations thus secured and used as a bribe, the matrons were assured quick service. Having in this

[55] The Petrograd Commune; the Moscow Commune.

manner provided themselves with 'influence' in the various departments, it did not matter if the managers in charge of the schools sabotaged their work, neglected and even abused the children, or often speculated with the provisions obtained for the inmates. They had 'friends on high.'

The results of this pleasant arrangement, universal in Russia, are obvious, of course. But my friend wouldn't be a party to such practices. She refused to add 'dead souls.' She knew that each dead soul was living on the already insignificant ration of some child. She declined to feed the numerous inspectors, examiners, and correctors of her district. The result was a long and bitter struggle against the vicious circle, a struggle which undermined her health and ended in her being ousted from her position, literally thrown out on the street. In vain she tried to call the attention of the 'comrade' at the head of the Petrograd Department of Education, Madam Lilina. She could not be seen, and she never visited the school of my friend. The 'show' schools took up all of her time. Besides, Madam Lilina would hardly have credited my friend's story. It is not customary to pay attention to 'outsiders' that make complaints against Communists. And, incidentally, it is a dangerous thing to indulge in.

Later I met Madam Lilina. I think she is sincere and very devoted to her work. But she is a bigot, without vision. She depends entirely upon her chief subordinates, all Communists, for her information about the conditions in the schools. The criterion of fitness and veracity in Russia is adherence to the Communist Party. It is hardly necessary to emphasise the result.

All this (the partial starvation of children in Bolshevik schools) I learned gradually, painfully, day by day. At first I refused to believe that the 'dead soul' method was a general practice. Next door to me, in the Hotel Astoria, 'First House of the Soviet,' lived a little woman and her two children. She was a Communist, but one who fought hard against the 'dead soul' method. She worked in various child institutions. She not only corroborated the condition I found at the school on Kronverski

Prospekt, but she took me to many others where the same practices prevailed.

Everywhere 'dead souls' lived off some of the half-starved children. My neighbour related the experience she had had with her own children, a boy of three and a girl of nine. Both had been placed in a colony. Out of her own meagre earnings the mother regularly sent the children extra provisions, as they did not get enough there. At the end of six months both children took sick and had to be removed to the one room they shared with their mother. The girl had developed a pernicious rash and the boy was badly run down. Both cases were diagnosed as due to malnutrition.

I became friends with my neighbour, a sincere and hardworking Communist. Through her I learned much of the general status of children. More and more I came to see that the Bolsheviks were trying to do all they could for the child, but that their efforts were being defeated by the parasitic bureaucracy their State had created. Above all proved destructive their notion that even the child must be used for propaganda purposes.

The 'show' schools were a most evil influence, especially on the children at large. They poisoned the child's mind with a sense of injustice and discrimination. For quicker and more correctly than the adult, the child senses wrong and sham. And while these 'show' schools were being used as newspaper copy abroad, the masses of children in Russia were neglected as the workers' children are in the rest of the world. Everywhere the privileged few receive all the advantages. Bolshevik Russia is not exempt from this cruel situation.

I have said in the beginning that I was deeply disturbed when I first heard that children were isolated as 'thieves and moral defectives.' At the time, I ascribed this attitude to the old-fashioned notion of the physician in charge at the Hotel de l'Europe. An article in the official *Pravda* and the talk I had with many leading Communists, among them Maxim Gorky, Madam Lilina, and others, convinced me that nearly all of them believed in 'inherent moral depravity.'

Some high-standing pedagogues even favoured prisons for such 'moral defectives.' But that was too much for Lunacharsky, the Commissar of Education, Gorky, and others of the more progressive element, whom orthodox Communists regard as sentimentalists. Lunacharsky fought the barbarous proposition and, fortunately, his side scored a victory. Yet even as late as September 1921, there were 200 juveniles, among them a child of eight, in the Taganka Prison of Moscow.

I am certain neither Lunacharsky nor Gorky knew about it. But therein lies the curse of the vicious circle; it makes it impossible for those at the head to know what the host of their subordinates are doing. The presence of the children in the Taganka was discovered by the political prisoners who had been sent there. They reported it to their friends on the outside, who took the matter up with Lunacharsky. The children were finally removed from the prison.

However, schools and colonies for the 'moral defectives' are not much better than a prison. An investigation made by a committee of the Communist Youth disclosed harrowing conditions in some of those schools in Petrograd. The report was published in the *Petrograd Pravda* of May 1920. It substantiated the charges frequently made – among them the general practices of 'dead souls,' the multiplication of attendants at the expense of the children's rations, and other methods of corruption and inefficiency. The committee found, for instance, 138 attendants in a school of 125 children. In another, 38 attendants to 25 children. These were not exceptional cases.

Besides that, the committee's report showed that the children were badly neglected, clad in dirty rags, and permitted to sleep on filthy, ill-smelling bedding without linen; that some children had been punished by being locked in dark rooms for the night, others forced to go without supper, and some had even been beaten. The report caused a great stir in official circles. A special investigation was ordered, and, of course, like similar things in America, it resulted in a whitewash. The committee of the Communist Youth was rebuked for 'exaggerating.' It was stated that the article in the *Pravda* should have never appeared, such stories are water on the mill of the counter-revolutionists, and so forth.

I discussed the matter with some Communists. How could such a thing happen in Soviet Russia? I received the stereotyped reply, 'lack of dependable and efficient workers.' I offered to take up work among the unfortunate children branded as 'moral defectives.' Oh, you must see Comrade Lilina,' I was advised. 'She will be delighted to have you.' Several days later Comrade Lilina called. She is a frail woman with a hard face, the typical New England school ma'am of fifty years ago. She assured me that she was intimately familiar with the best methods of pedagogy and psychology. I ventured to tell her that I did not believe in the theory of the moral depravity of children, and that no modern educator held such antiquated notions; that even defective children could not be punished or be branded moral degenerates.

I told her of the modern methods and of the experimental work with delinquent children done in America by Judge Lindsey and others who had repudiated the moralistic conception of sinner and saint. Oh, yes, that was all very well in a capitalistic country where food and everything else was plentiful, but in starved Russia 'moral defectives' were the inevitable result of long war, revolution, and hunger.

The interview convinced me that if I were to take up work among the little victims my efforts would be thwarted at every step by this prim and dogmatic lady. She in her turn probably thought that it would not be safe to entrust the care of children in the Communist State to an Anarchist. At any rate, nothing came of the project.

I give this as an illustration of the falsity of the oft-repeated Bolshevik claim that the corruption, abuse, and inefficiency of their regime are due to the lack of dependable workers. During my stay in Russia I came in contact with a surprisingly large number of persons able and willing to co-operate in the educational, economic, and other non-political work. Not being Communist, however, they are discriminated against, discouraged and surrounded by a spying system that makes all initiative and effort futile.

During my four months' travel through the Ukraine I had ample opportunity to visit crèches, kindergartens, boarding schools, and colonies –unofficially, of course. Everywhere I found the same situation: a model 'show' school with well-fed and well-cared-for children, while in the other institutions the children were hungry. Often, I saw how the men and women in charge were beating their wings against the bureaucratic machine, earnestly striving to defend the interests of the children; but striving in vain, only to be finally eliminated by the all-powerful machine.

I saw a striking illustration of this phase in Moscow shortly before I left. In a certain district, there is a model crèche, the best organised and equipped I came across in Russia. The matron was a very rare type of womanhood, an idealist, an educator of long experience, and a tireless worker. She set herself sternly against the 'dead soul' practice. She would not rob Peter to feed Paul. She would not bribe the petty officials of the sub-department.

As usual, a campaign was started against her. The leading spirit in the miserable attack was the physician of the crèche, a Communist. All sorts of accusations were laid at the matron's door, none of which had any basis. But the machine would not let up until the woman was forced out of the place. Incidentally, that meant also being deprived of her room. The woman was the mother of a four-month-old baby.

It was in November, the weather was cold, the damp penetrating. Yet the matron who had fought for the crèche was ordered to leave the crèche. For the sake of her infant she refused to go until assured of a room in the building. She was then given a little, dark, damp room in a basement which could not have been heated for three years. In that tomb the infant fell sick and has been ailing ever since.

Does Lunacharsky know of such cases? Do the leading Communists know? Some no doubt do. But they are too busy with 'important State affairs.' And they have become callous to all such 'trifles.' Then, too, they themselves are caught in the vicious circle, in the machinery of Bolshevik officialdom. They know that adherence to the party covers a multitude of sins.

During my two years' stay in Russia I visited many institutions, but I met very few happy children. In all that time, I heard a really hearty child's laugh only once, in Archangel. I may have occasion to write about that experience in a future article. On the whole, most children in Bolshevik institutions impressed me as colourless and stereotyped, veritable children of orphan asylums.

There is something practically gripping about those children. They are not only starved for food, but even more so for affection – they are lonely children. I know this does not correspond with the legends circulated of the millennium come to the child in Bolshevik Russia. But, then, I have no intention of perpetuating legends.

There was one other factor which set the Communist State above the other Governments – the abolition of child labour. That was its most significant achievement, for which the Communists deserved much credit. But now that Lenin's new economic policy is fast resurrecting the dead, now that capitalism and private exploitation are slowly but surely returning to Russia, the Bolshevik Government will soon be the 'equal' of all other civilised Governments, with child labour as its great source of national wealth.

A Visit to Peter Kropotkin

Among those I wanted to see most when I reached Russia in January 1920, was Peter Alexeivitch Kropotkin. I immediately made inquiries how to reach him. I was informed that I could do so only when I got to Moscow, as Kropotkin lived in Dmitrov, a small town 60 versts [40 miles] from the city. Now, one does not travel at will in a country so stricken by war and revolution as Russia — a country where the State is in absolute control of every breath of life. There was nothing to do but wait until I would be given the chance to go to Moscow. Fortunately, that opportunity soon presented itself.

Early in March a number of prominent Communists went to Moscow, among them Radek and Gorky. I was permitted to go in the same car. When I reached Moscow, I began to look about for means to reach Dmitrov. But again there was a delay. I learned that it was almost impossible to travel the ordinary way. Typhus was then raging. The railroad stations were overcrowded with people lying around for days and weeks. There was always a savage scramble for an inch of space. Five hundred unfortunate beings would crowd into a car that had room only for fifty. Starved and worn out, they would crowd even on the roof and platform of the car, unmindful of the biting frost or the imminent danger of being thrown off. Not a journey but some of the victims froze to death — others hurled from the speeding train.

I was in despair, for I had heard Kropotkin was ailing that winter. I feared he might not live until spring. I would not ask to be given a special car; neither could I muster up courage to go the ordinary way. An unforeseen circumstance came to my rescue. The editor of the *London Herald*, accompanied by one of his reporters, had preceded me to Moscow. They also wanted to visit Kropotkin, and they had been given a special car. Together with Alexander Berkman and A. [Alexander] Shapiro I was able to join Mr. Lansbury and make the trip in comparative safety. The journey was made in fairly good time; it was a starry night, and the whole country was one vast sheet of snow. Our footsteps resounded in the silence of the village asleep.

The Kropotkin cottage stood back in the garden away from the street. Only a faint ray from a kerosene lamp lit up the path leading to the house. I afterward learned that kerosene was scarce in the Kropotkin household, and light had to be economised. After Peter had finished his day's work the lamp would be used in the living room, where the family gathered in the evening. We were warmly received by Sophie Kropotkin and the daughter, and taken to the room where we found the Grand Old Man.

The last time I had seen him was in 1907, in Paris, which I had visited after the Anarchist Congress at Amsterdam. Kropotkin, for many years barred from France, had just been given the right to return. He was at that time already sixty-five years of age; but he looked so full of vitality, was so alert, that he seemed much younger. He was a great inspiration to all of us who were fortunate to come in close contact with him.

Somehow one could never think of Peter Alexeivitch as being old. Not so in March 1920. I was shocked by his altered appearance. He was fearfully emaciated. He received us with the graciousness that was so characteristic of him. We felt from the very beginning that our visit would not be satisfactory; Peter would not be able to talk freely with us in the presence of two strangers, journalists at that. But we had to make the best of the situation. After an hour's talk, we asked Mrs. Kropotkin and Sasha to entertain the English guests while we conversed with Kropotkin in Russian.

Aside from my concern in his health I was eager to get some light from him on the vital questions that had already begun to trouble my mind — the relation of the Bolsheviks to the Revolution; the despotic methods which, as everybody had assured me, had been imposed upon the ruling party by intervention and the blockade. What was Kropotkin's opinion about it, and how explain his long silence?

I had taken no notes, and I can give only the gist of our brief talk. It was to the effect that the Russian Revolution had carried the people to great heights and had paved the way for profound social changes. Had the people then been permitted to utilise their released energies, Russia would not now be in her ruined condition. The Bolsheviks, who had been swept to the fore by the gigantic revolutionary wave, had at first caught the popular ear by extreme revolutionary slogans. Thus, they gained the confidence of the masses and the support of the militant revolutionists.

Early in the October period the Bolsheviks began to subordinate the interests of the Revolution to the building up of their dictatorship. It coerced and paralysed every social activity. Kropotkin referred to the co-operatives as the main medium which, in his opinion, could have bridged the interests of the peasants and the workers. But it was these very co-operatives which were among the first to be crushed.

He spoke with much heat of the depression, the persecution, the cruel hounding of every political shade of opinion, and he cited numerous examples of the misery and distress of the people. Above all, he was most emphatic against the Bolshevik Government for having thus discredited Socialism and Communism in the eyes of the Russian people. It was a heart-breaking picture which Kropotkin unrolled before us that evening.

Why, then, had he not raised his voice against these evils, against the machine which was sapping the life-blood from the Revolution? Kropotkin gave two reasons: first, because so long as Russia was being attacked by the combined imperialists of Europe, and Russian women and children were starved to death by the criminal blockade, he could not join the shrieking chorus of the ex-revolutionists in the cry of 'Crucify!' He preferred to keep silent for the present.

Secondly, there was no medium of expression in Russia itself, hence no way of reaching the people. To protest to the Government was useless. Its concern was to maintain its power at any cost. It could, therefore, not stop at such trifles as human life or human rights. But then, he added, 'We have always pointed out the blessings of Marxism in action. Why now be surprised?'

I asked whether he was noting down his impressions and observations. Surely, he must see the importance of such a record to his comrades, to the workers; in fact, to the whole world. Kropotkin looked at me for a moment, then said:

No, I do not write. It is impossible to write when one is in the midst of great human suffering and distress, when every hour brings new tales of woe which one may not ameliorate. Besides, all personal privacy and safety have been destroyed. There may be a raid any moment – the Cheka comes swooping down in the night, ransacks every corner of the house, turns everything upside down, and marches off with every scrap of paper.

Under such constant stress, it is impossible to keep records. But more than all these considerations is my book on ethics. I can work only a few hours a day, and I still have much to do. I must therefore concentrate on that to the exclusion of everything else.

We had already monopolised our comrade too long. Though there was still much to talk about, we had to content ourselves for that evening. The conversation again became general. But it was getting late, and our host was fatigued. Soon we took our leave. We agreed to come back in the spring, when we should have more time to talk over matters.

After a tender embrace, which Peter never failed to give those he loved, we returned to our car. My heart was heavy with the great Russian tragedy, my spirit confused and troubled by what I had heard. I was also distressed by the physical condition of our comrade. I feared he could not survive until the spring. The winter of 1920 had been most terrible. People had been dying from typhus, hunger, and cold. The thought that Peter Kropotkin might go to his grave, and the world never know what he thought of the Russian Revolution, was appalling.

I felt somewhat impatient. Kropotkin had braved the despotism of the Tsars and the raids of their political Okhrana. Why could he not write now? It was just like the old: they for ever dwell in the past while the present passes them by. It was only much later that I understood why Kropotkin had been unable to write about the events in Russia.

In July 1920, I again came to Moscow. I was with the expedition of the Museum of the Revolution on the way to the Ukraine. One day Sasha Kropotkin called me up. She had obtained an auto, from one of the Government officials, and would Alexander Berkman and I go out to Dmitrov? The next

Kropotkin's Funeral

Outside Dmitrov railway station

A banner with the words: 'We demand the release of all the imprisoned anarchists who are fighting for the same ideas for which Kropotkin fought – for Anarchy.'

day we started out, reaching Dmitrov in a few hours. The garden surrounding the Kropotkin house was full of bloom, completely hiding the cottage from view. Peter was having his afternoon nap, but he rose as soon as he heard our voices. He joined us; he had improved marvellously; he was so alert, so active, so energetic. He immediately took us to the vegetable garden, which was almost entirely Sophie Kropotkin's work, Peter's pride, and the chief support of the family. He took great delight in showing us a new species of lettuce which Sophie had grown, having large heads like cabbage, with leaves of fragrant green. 'You must have some for dinner,' said Peter jovially. The spring had certainly wrought a miracle in him. He was a different man.

The first seven months of my stay in Russia had almost crushed me. I had come with so much enthusiasm, with a passionate desire to throw myself into the work, into the holy defence of the Revolution. What I found completely overwhelmed me. I was unable to do anything. The chariot wheel of the Socialist State rolled over me, paralysing my energy. The wretchedness and distress of the people, the callous disregard of their needs, the persecution and the repressions tore at my mind and heart, and made life unbearable.

Was it the Revolution which had turned idealists into wild beasts? If so, the Bolsheviks were mere pawns in the hands of the inevitable. Or was it the cold, impersonal character of the State which by foul means had harnessed the revolution to its cart and was now whipping it into channels indispensable to the State? I could not answer these questions. Not in July 1920, at any rate. Perhaps Kropotkin could.

Kropotkin on the Russian Revolution

During the second visit to Peter Kropotkin we had an hour together. In that time, Peter spoke in detail of the Russian Revolution, the part played by the Bolsheviks, the lesson to the Anarchists in particular and the world in general. He considered the Russian Revolution in scope and possibilities greater than the French Revolution. While it is true that the people were not developed in the Western sense, yet they are more responsive to new arrangements of life. The spirit of the masses during the February and October Revolutions demonstrated that they understood the great changes waiting their concerted efforts, and they were willing to do their share.

The people knew that something tremendous was before them, which they themselves must face, organise, and direct. That spirit, though now fettered by hunger, privation, and persecution, is yet very much alive. The dogged resistance offered by the people of Russia to the Bolshevik yoke is the best proof of that. The Bolsheviks in their march to power were far from being the advance guard of the revolution, as they claim. On the contrary, they were the dam which had thrown back the rising tide of the people's energies.

In their fixed idea that only a dictatorship can direct and protect the revolution, they went about strengthening their formidable State which is now crushing the revolution. As Marxists, they never have, nor will they ever realise that the only protection of the revolution lies in the ability of the people to organise their own economic life. For the rest, Kropotkin added, he had set forth his views on the Russian Revolution in his letter to the workers of Europe, which was, I believe, widely published.

Kropotkin also spoke of the part the Anarchists played in the revolution, of the death of some, the heroic struggle of many, the irresponsibility of the few. Above all, he emphasised the need for all the Anarchists to be better equipped for reconstructive work during the revolution. I distinctly remember these words:

We Anarchists have talked much about the Social Revolution. But how many had ever taken pains to prepare for the actual work during and after the revolution? The Russian Revolution has demonstrated the imperativeness of such preparation for practical reconstructive work.

In a letter to one of his closest friends Kropotkin wrote that he had come to see in Syndicalism the economic basis of Anarchism. In other words, the medium for the economic organisation and expression of the energies, of the people during the revolutionary period.

It was a memorable day. Alas! the last I was ever to spend with our Grand Old Man. When I was called to take care of him during his last illness I reached Dmitrov an hour after his death. The usual bureaucratic confusion, inefficiency, and delay robbed me of the opportunity to render Kropotkin some slight service in return for all that he had given me

Two things had struck me in Kropotkin on both visits: the lack of bitterness toward the Bolsheviks and the fact that he never once alluded to his own hardships and privations. It was only after his death that I learned a few details of his life under the Bolshevik regime. In the early part of 1918 Kropotkin had grouped around him some of the ablest specialists in various branches of political economy. The purpose was to make a careful study of the economic resources of Russia, and to compile these resources in monographs, to make them of practical help in the reconstruction of Russia.

Kropotkin was the editor-in-chief of that undertaking. One volume was prepared, but never published. The Federalist League, as this scientific group was known, was broken up by the Government and all the material confiscated.

On two occasions the Kropotkin apartments were requisitioned and the family forced to find other quarters. It was after all these experiences that the Kropotkins moved to Dmitrov, where he became an involuntary exile. Even in the summer it was difficult to visit him. Special permission had to be procured to travel, and that involved much effort and time. In the winter, it was almost altogether impossible. Thus he, who had in the past gathered at his home the best in thought and ideas from every land, was now forced to the life of a recluse.

His only visitors were unfortunate peasants, workers of his village, and some of the intelligentsia who would come to him with their daily misfortunes. I remember that the evening of our visit Kropotkin had received a letter from an old friend in Moscow, a scientist. The man was living with his wife and two children in one room. Only a small lamp was lighting up the family table at which the children had to prepare their lesson, the wife copy some manuscripts, while he used one corner to do his scientific research. He was employed at a place twelve versts [eight miles] from home, and had to walk that daily

Kropotkin, who had always kept in touch with the world through numerous publications in every tongue, was now cut off entirely from that source of life. He was not even able to learn what was happening in Moscow or Petrograd. His only channel of news were the two government papers, *Pravda* and *Izvestiya*. He was much handicapped in his work on ethics while he lived in Dmitrov. He could not obtain the necessary books of research. In short, Kropotkin was mentally starved, which was, no doubt, greater torture to him than physical malnutrition. He received a much better payok, or ration, than most people; but even that was by far not sufficient to keep up his vitality.

Fortunately, he received from time to time assistance – in the form of provisions – from various sources. Thus, his comrades from abroad, as well as those from the Ukraine, often sent him foodstuffs. He also received similar gifts from Makhno, then heralded by the Bolsheviks as the terror of the counter-revolutionary forces in Southern Russia. But especially was felt the lack of light and fuel. When I visited the Kropotkins in 1920, they were considering themselves fortunate to have light in more than one room. During part of 1918 and all of 1919, Kropotkin wrote his ethics by the flicker of a tiny oil lamp that nearly blinded him.

During the short hours of the day he would transcribe his notes on a typewriter, slowly and painfully pounding out every letter. However, it was not his own discomfort which sapped Kropotkin's strength. It was the hardships of Russia, the suffering about him, the suppression of every thought, the persecution and imprisonment for opinion sake, the endless *raztrels* of people, which made his last years the deepest tragedy.

If only he could have done something to help, to lessen the suffering, to bring the dictators of Russia to their senses. But he could not. He could not, like some of the old revolutionary guard, make common cause with the enemies of the revolution. Even had he found a way of having his protests published in the European Press, the reactionaries would have used them against Russia. No, he could not do that. And he knew only too well that it was useless to protest to the Bolshevik Government.

Yet, so great was his anguish, that on two occasions Peter Kropotkin addressed himself to that deaf ear. Once in protest against the terrible practice of taking hostages; the other time against the complete suppression of publishing undertakings other than the State's.

Ever since the Cheka began its sinister existence, the Bolshevik Government had sanctioned the taking of hostages. Old and young, mothers, fathers, sisters, brothers, even children, had been held and often shot for the offence of one of their own — offences which, in nine cases out of ten, they knew nothing about.

In the fall of 1920, the Social-Revolutionists that emigrated to Europe threatened retaliation if the repressions against their comrades continued. The Bolshevik Government announced in its official press that for every Communist it would take ten Social-Revolutionists. It was then that the famous revolutionist, Vera N. Figner, and Peter Kropotkin sent a protest to the powers that be. They pointed out that the practice of taking hostages was a blot on the Russian Revolution, an evil which had already brought terrible results in its wake, that the future would never forgive them for such a barbaric method.

The second protest was made in reply to the attempt the Government was making at 'liquidating' all publishing undertakings, whether political, co-operative, or private. This protest was addressed to the President of the then sitting Eighth All-Russian Congress of Soviets. It is interesting to note that Gorky, himself an official of the Commissariat of Education, had sent almost on the same day from Petrograd a similar protest.

Kropotkin, in his statement, called attention to the danger of such a policy to all progress; in fact, to all thought. Such

State monopoly on thought would make creative work utterly impossible. The situation in Russia during the last four years has given ample proof of that.

One of the striking characteristics of Peter Kropotkin was his reticence in everything concerning himself. In my stay of thirty-six hours at his Dmitrov home, while his body lay in death, I learned more of his personal life than during all the years I had known him. But few even of his immediate circle knew that Peter Alexeivitch was an artist and a musician of considerable talent. Among his effects I discovered a whole collection of his drawings of great merit.

He loved music passionately, and was himself a musician of no mean ability. He spent much of his leisure moments at the piano. No doubt he was able to find some forgetfulness and peace in the masters whose works he rendered with deep understanding.

He lay in his workroom as if peacefully asleep, his face as tender in death as it had been in life. There he lay, this great son of Russia. Through strife and stress he had remained true to the Revolution, and would not forsake it. He did not live to see Capitalism in Russia erected as a monument upon the grave of the Revolution. But even that would not have robbed him of his fervent faith in the resurrection of the people, the ultimate triumph of a Libertarian Revolution.

The Trade Unions

The much-praised achievement of the Bolsheviks in the matter of trade unions reminds me of Mrs. Alving's remark in Ibsen's *Ghosts*: 'I only wished to pick at a single knot, but when I got that undone the whole thing ravelled out. And then I understood that it was all machine-sewn.'

Among the first things called to one's attention when one arrives in Russia are the trade unions. Think of it, seven million workers organised into one body, having their magnificent labour temples, their educational and cultural courses, their grand meetings and concerts. What other country can make such a showing? You are overwhelmed. But no sooner do you begin to pick at one knot when the whole seam ravels out. You come to see that trade unions, more than any other Bolshevik institution, are machine-sewn — sewn by the machine of the Communist State.

In fact, it is most confusing to talk of trade unions under the Bolshevik regime. After all, trade unions have a definite historic meaning, at least to workers outside Bolshevik Russia. They represent, in their conservative sense even, the fighting arena of organised labour for economic improvement. In the revolutionary sense the trade unions, or rather the Industrial and Syndicalist Unions, are the economic training school of the militant masses for the overthrow of exploitation and the management by the workers of production in a liberated society.

Yet neither in the conservative nor even in the revolutionary sense do the trade unions represent in Russia the needs of the workers. What they really are is the coerced and militarised adjunct of the Bolshevik State. They are 'the school of Communism,' as Lenin insisted in his thesis on the functions of trade unions But, they are not even that. A school presupposes the free expression and initiative of the pupils, whereas the trade unions in Russia are military barracks for the mobilised labour army, forced into membership by the whip of the State driver.

The trade unions in Russia, though young in years (they came into being in 1905), were very militant organisations. They had to be in order to withstand the cruel persecution under the Tsar. But though they led an underground existence most of the time, they were none the less an important factor in the economic struggles of the Russian worker. That fact was demonstrated forcibly early after the February revolution.

The trade unions, imbued with the new spirit that had come to Russia, were not content with mere political changes. Their aim was to get the workers in possession of the economic structure of the country. Even before the workers expropriated the shops and factories the trade unions had organised shop and factory committees for the control of the industrial life of the community.

These committees later gave way to the All-Russian Trade Union Soviet, which worked in close union with the other Soviets. In other words, the trade unions were, even before the Bolshevik regime, the organised expression of the demands and aspirations of the workers. Thus, the third Conference of Trade Unions, held in Petrograd in July, 1917, already sent 210 delegates representing a membership of 1,475,425.

The advent of the 'Dictatorship of the Proletariat' quickly made itself felt in the trade unions. Adherence to labour organisations became compulsory, everyone who worked being automatically enrolled in the union and compelled to pay for the pleasure, whether he enjoyed it or not. The 3 per cent dues were simply deducted from his wage, so that the Russian worker had to stand the cost of the very organisations which destroyed every symptom of initiative and self-direction in the Russian trade unions.

The All-Russian Trade Union Soviet consists of 120 members. Its Central Executive Committee has eleven members, and practically only communists can get elected to either body. The result is that the trade unions have become a mere branch of the state machinery, completely controlled and directed by the latter in its policies and functions. The average member has no say whatever in the activities of his organisation, nor are regular meetings of the union held, in the Western sense, except such as are thoroughly dominated and managed by the Bolshevik faction in each union. If any union should venture to exercise the function of a real union it is quickly given to understand that, whatever trade unions may do in Western Europe or America, in the Communist State they must obey the law and keep their mouths shut.

To illustrate: the bakers of Moscow, representing a large and militant Union, went on strike in the summer of 1920 for an increase of their bread allowance. The Government did not trouble itself much about the matter. The striking local was simply dissolved, its leaders expelled, and some of the most active members arrested. The more prominent of the spokesmen of the strikers were forbidden to participate in any union gatherings and deprived of the right to hold office.

Similar tactics were followed by the Bolsheviks in various other strikes. An interesting incident of this character was the Moscow printers' difficulty. In their case, it was not even a strike; it was merely the 'impudence' of having called a meeting to which members of the British Labour Mission, then in Moscow, were invited.

At that meeting Chernov, leader of the Social Revolutionists, and Dan, a prominent Menshevik, committed the unpardonable sin of telling the British Labour men a few facts about the trade union and labour conditions in Russia. Immediately after that all the officials of the Printers' Union were suspended and some of them thrown into jail. Throughout the country, in all official papers, the Moscow printers were heralded as counter-revolutionists, traitors, and 'skinners of labour,' and denounced in bitterest terms that served to awe and terrorise the rest of the proletariat of the country.

So, absolute and crushing is the tyranny over the trade unions that the least protest is denounced as a breach of revolutionary and labour discipline and a crime against the Revolution. When, during the Petrograd strikes of 1921, the workers of the Baltic shops protested against the arrest of twenty-two of their members, they were told by Antselovitch, the chairman of the Petrograd Trade Unions, that they all belonged in the Cheka, and several days later a raid took place at the shops, resulting in the arrest of numerous workers.

In short, the trade unions in Bolshevik Russia have been entirely absorbed by the State and have no other meaning or function than to do police duty for the State. Naturally, such conditions could not last very long without arousing the most bitter discontent on the part of the workers. In fact, in 1920 this discontent became so general and threatening that the Government saw itself compelled to give serious consideration to the situation. The issue of the functions of the trade unions was taken up by the end of 1920, and it soon became apparent that even within the Communist Party itself there raged conflicting views on that important question.

All the leading Communists participated in the heated verbal contest which was to decide the fate of the trade unions. The theses presented disclosed four main tendencies.

- First, the Lenin-Zinoviev faction, which held that 'the trade unions have only one function under the Proletarian Dictatorship' — that is, to serve as schools of Communism.
- The second tendency was represented by Riazanov and his adherents, who insisted that the trade unions must continue to function as the forum of the workers and their economic protector.
- The third faction was that of Trotsky, the military genius who can think only in terms of militarism. He advanced the thesis that the trade unions will in time become the managers and controllers of the industries, but that for the present the Union management must be appointed by military methods.
- Last, and most important, was the Workers' Opposition led by Madam Kollontai and Shlyapnikov, who really represented the actual sentiment of the workers and had their support. This Opposition insisted that the militarisation of the trade unions had destroyed the interest of the workers in the economic reconstruction of the country and paralysed their productive capacity. They demanded the liberation of the masses from the yoke of the bureaucratic State and its corrupt officialdom, and giving the people opportunity for the exercise of their creative energies. They pointed out that the October Revolution had been fought to enable the masses to be in control of the industrial life of the country. In short, the Workers' Opposition voiced the accumulated protest and discontent of the rank and file.

It was a battle royal, with Trotsky and Zinoviev chasing each other over the country, in separate special trains, to disprove each other's contentions. In Petrograd, for instance, Zinoviev's influence was so powerful that it required a big struggle before Trotsky received permission to address the Communist local on his views about the controversy.

The latter engendered intense feeling and came near disrupting the Communist Party. But God loves Lenin. Always when his structure begins to totter the Lord sends him some prop. The great labour unrest and numerous strikes in Petrograd in February 1921, and the Kronstadt insurrection proved that prop. Communist unity was to be maintained at all cost. And so the 'Little Father' took his unruly children, one by one, and taught them their manners.

Lenin denounced the Workers' Opposition as Anarcho-Syndicalist, middle-class ideology, and ordered its suppression. Schlyapnikov, one of the Opposition's most influential leaders, was referred to by Lenin as a 'peeved Commissar,' and was subsequently silenced by being made a member of the Central Committee of the Communist Party. Madam Kollontai was told to hold her tongue or get out of the party, and her pamphlet — setting forth the views of the Opposition — was suppressed.

Some of the lesser lights of the Workers' Opposition were given a vacation in the Cheka, and even Riazanov – an old and tried Communist – was suspended for six months from all [trade] union activities. As to Trotsky, whom Lenin held up to the party's scorn as an 'ignoramus in fundamental Marxism,' he was hustled off to Kronstadt to bring there the 'peace of Warsaw.' Lenin and his saint, Juste [trusty] Zinoviev, scored a victory. The trade unions remained the 'school for Communism.'

The New Economic Policy is fast reshaping the whole structure of Russia. The trade unions are among the first to feel its effects. At a session of the Central Committee of the Communist Party, held in Moscow in December 1921, the functions of the trade unions under the new economic policy was discussed. A commission consisting of Lenin, Radzutak,[***] and Andreyev[†††] was chosen to prepare a thesis on the subject.

[***] V E Radzutak was a Bolshevik politician.
[†††] A A Andreyev supported Trotsky at this time.

Later their thesis was accepted, as usual, unanimously by the All-Russian Central Soviet of Trade Unions.

The thesis speaks volumes for Lenin's capacity to shed his skin. Among other things it contains the following:

(1) Compulsory enrolment of the workers in the labour organisations brought about bureaucratic deterioration of the trade unions and alienated them from the masses (for saying the same things many workers had been denounced as counter-revolutionists and 'skinners' and were sent to the Cheka); it is therefore now necessary to establish voluntary membership in the unions.

(2) The workers joining unions must not be interfered with or harassed on account of their political or religious faith. (Shades of the numerous victims who were discriminated against and browbeaten because of their political views unsympathetic to the Bolsheviks!)

(3) The economic reconstruction of Russia necessitates the strictest concentration of power in the hands of individual management; therefore, the labour unions must not seek to control the industries leased or owned by private capitalists.

It is evident that the New Economic Policy, supported by Lenin's thesis on the role of the unions, is opening the door to new labour problems and inevitable conflicts. The settling of all coming labour conflicts will be in the hands of a 'higher body,' outside of the trade unions. Lenin's commission has already indicated that this 'highest authority' of forced arbitration of labour disputes is to be no other than the Communist Party and the Third International.

It is apparent that the Communist International means to preserve its domination of the Labour movement of Russia, while it is at the same time bending every effort to gain control of the labour organisations in Western Europe and America.

Meanwhile the Russian worker, under the new economic policy is faring even worse than since the Revolution began. He has lost even those guarantees, few as they were, that accrued to him as a result of the revolutionary changes. Especially is this true in regard to the hours of work. The eight-hour day, practically universal in Russia for the last four years, has now been abolished de facto. According to the official organ, the *Moscow Pravda*, of December 1921, the situation is as follows: only 86 out of 695 industrial establishments have retained the eight-hour day. In most of the others work continues nine hours; in 44 establishments, the workday is ten to twelve hours long; in 11, fourteen to sixteen hours; in 44 workshops, no regular hours exist. Even children have been found, in some places, to work twelve to fourteen hours. The bakers are the most exploited and work longest hours, from twelve to eighteen.

These data refer to conditions in Moscow, the capital of Russia. In the provinces, the situation is even worse. Thus, in the Don coal district the miners remain at work sixteen to seventeen continuous hours. In the State leather factory in Vitebsk twelve hours constitutes the normal workday; in the Astrakhan fisheries, according to the local representative at the Second All-Russian Conference for the Protection of Labour, the workday is virtually unlimited.

It can be thus seen how the new policy of State and private capitalism is showering its blessings on the Russian worker.

The Russian Revolution, however, has not been entirely in vain. It has uprooted many of the old notions of the Russian masses, and the worker is no longer the docile slave he used to be. He has been fed on politics ad nauseam; he no longer believes in it. Now that he will be able to combine with his fellows in new Labour organisations he will no doubt try more direct methods to assert himself.

Lenin and his retinue are sensing the danger. Their attack upon and the persecution of the Workers' Opposition and the Anarcho-Syndicalists are continuing with even greater intensity. Is it that the Anarcho-Syndicalist star is rising in the East? Who knows – Russia is the land of miracles.

NOTES

1 Published by Freedom Press, London, in 1922, (not including the introduction).
2 *Redención* (Alcoy), No. 91, 7 December 1922.
3 Emma Goldman, *Living My Life*, New York: Dover Publications, 1970, Vol. 2., pp. 968-72.
4 There is a You-tube clip on the funeral of Kropotkin online: https://www.youtube.com/watch?v=Rt4SFsmOvlk

Notes on the Authors

Armando Borghi (1882-1968) was active in the Italian anarchist movement from an early age, and subsequently worked in Bologna for the Construction Union. He was a key figure in the Italian Syndicalist Union (USI). He was imprisoned for over nine months after his return to Italy from Russia in October 1920.[1] He lived for many years outside Italy, both before the First World War and while the Fascists were in power. He returned to Italy after the end of the Second World War. He wrote an historical autobiography: *Mezzo secolo di anarchia (1898-1945)*.

Emma Goldman was born in 1869 in Kovno (Kaunas), a Lithuanian city then part of the Russian Empire. She was a textile worker, nurse, journalist, anti-militarist, and a lecturer on family planning, feminism and anarchism. She and her partner, Alexander Berkman, were once described by J. Edgar Hoover as 'beyond doubt, two of the most dangerous anarchists in this country'. She and two hundred other 'dangerous aliens' were expelled from the USA, on the *Buford*, leaving New York harbour on 21 December 1919, bound for Russia. She travelled widely working to find objects for a Museum of the Revolution. Goldman and Berkman were shocked by the events and reprisal killings carried out by the Bolshevik government in and after the Kronstadt revolt of March 1921. She left Russia in December and settled for a time in Britain. Later, after 1936, she worked for the CNT and supported anarchists in Spain. She died in Toronto in 1940. Her writings include: *My Disillusionment in Russia*, *My Further Disillusionment in Russia*. (New York: 1923 and 1924), and an autobiography: *Living My Life*, (New York, 1931).

'**Gaston Leval**' (Pierre Robert Piller, 1895-1978), left France for Spain in 1915 to avoid military service and joined the Spanish National Labour Confederation (the CNT). He was a delegate[2] to the congress of the Red Trade Union International (Profintern) meeting in Moscow in July 1921. He left Russia and recorded his conclusions in 'Choses de Russie', in *Le Libertaire*, (11-17 November 1921) these writings helped form his report to the CNT congress in Zaragoza in 1922. He also wrote about imprisoned anarchists. In 1924, he travelled to Argentina, returning to Spain before the outbreak of the civil war. His most valuable book, *Collectives in the Spanish Revolution*, was published in 1945.

Ángel Pestaña Núñez, (1886-1937) became the chief editor of the *Solidaridad Obrera*,[3] in 1918. In December 1919, the congress of the CNT (National Labour Confederation)[4] decided ' ... firstly, that it firmly defends the principles of the First International as defended by Bakunin, and secondly that it affiliates provisionally with the Communist International ...'[5] Pestaña travelled to Russia in the summer of 1920.[6] He interviewed Solomon Lozovsky and many other communists. He attended meeting of the newly formed Communist International,[7] but was disenchanted by its procedures.[8] Pestaña's report back to the CNT was delayed by a spell in prison, but eventually he was instrumental in persuading the CNT to break relations with Moscow. He was lucky to escape assassination in August 1922, but was seriously wounded. He remained a CNT leader for many year and founded a Syndicalist Party shortly before the outbreak of the Spanish Civil War. He wrote extensively on his experiences in Russia: *Consideraciones y juicios acerca de la Tercera Internacional*, ('Perspectives and judgements on the Third International') (Barcelona, 1922) was later re-worked and published in 1924 as *Setenta días en Rusia. Lo que yo vi*, ('Seventy days in Russia: what I saw'), from which the extract above has been drawn. He also published a second book: *Setenta días en Rusia. Lo que yo pienso.* ('Seventy days in Russia: what I think').

'**Vilkens**' (Manuel Fernández Álvarez, 1897-1936) Manuel Fernandez Álvarez used several aliases, including Alvar, Jack Wilkens, Iván Vilkens, Jaime Salán, and J. Galán. He was given a mandate in June 1920 to travel to Russia and report back.[9] He wrote a series of articles – first published in French in *Le Libertaire* (Paris) and later in Spanish in *La Antorcha* (Buenos Aires) – with the byline 'Vilkens, trade-union member and carpenter'. He wrote for *Pravda* and very briefly joined the Red Army.[10] He was in touch with the national committee of the CNT[11] and was a member of the CGT construction union in Chauny. He was a member, and later the secretary,[12] of a Spanish language revolutionary syndicalist network in France,[13] and as such attended meetings with other revolutionary syndicalists in Berlin in 1920 and 1921.[14] He also attended the meeting celebrating the 50th anniversary of the St Imier congress of 1872 (held in Bienne in September 1922). He was expelled from France, and later made a living in the film industry. In 1931, he was a delegate to the CNT's national congress in Madrid. He became a journalist on the *Heraldo de Madrid* and was killed early in the Spanish Civil War, in July 1936.[15]

NOTES

1   *Guerra di classe*, 25 September 1920, carries notes on Borghi's return from Russia and the text, dated 16.8.1920, of 'Documents of our mission in Russia', by Borghi. http://bibliotecaborghi.org/wp/wp-content/uploads/2016/01/Guerra-di-Classe_25set1920.pdf

2   Other Spanish delegates were ready to adapt to Bolshevik priorities, Leval was recalcitrant. He commented that three other delegates were secret members of the CP and had abused the confidence of CNT members at the national plenum which had chosen them. Xavier P Anlagua, 'La Visió de Gaston Leval de la Rússia Sovietica el 1921', *Recerques*, No. 3, Barcelona: Ariel, 1974, p. 205, refering to Gaston Leval, 'Circuit d'un destin'.

3   *Solidaridad Obrera*, (Labour Solidarity) was the daily paper of the CNT, published in Barcelona.

4   By 1919 the CNT had grown and had a membership of almost 800,000; its rival the UGT had some 210,000 members.

5   https://es.wikisource.org/wiki/II_Congreso_de_la_CNT

NOTES ON THE AUTHORS

6   He was in Russia from 26 June to 6 September.

7   The background and circumstances of this journey are described in Jason Garner, 'Separated by an "Ideological Chasm": The Spanish National Labour Confederation and Bolshevik Internationalism, 1917-1922', *Contemporary European History*, Vol. 15, No. 3, 2006. After leaving Russia Pestaña was imprisoned, first in Italy and then in Spain, so his report back to the CNT was delayed. The CNT withdrew from the Communist International and joined the re-formed (Berlin-based) syndicalist International Worker's Association.

8   See: Reiner Tosstorff, 'Mission Impossible: Ángel Pestaña's Encounter as CNT Delegate with the Bolshevik Revolution in 1920' in David Berry & Constance Bantman, Eds, *New Perspectives on Anarchism, Labour and Syndicalism: The Individual, the National and the Transnational*, Newcastle on Tyne: Cambridge Scholars Publishing, 2010.

9   Wayne Thorpe, *'The Workers Themselves'*: revolutionary syndicalism and international labour, 1913-1923, Dordrecht: Kluwer, 1989, pp. 177-78.

10   *Le Libertaire*, 1 April 1921; and the editions of 18 and 25 February 1921, contained his critique of the Red Army. He saw it as an army like any other; there were glaring differences in each ranks' powers, facilities and conditions. Ordinary soldiers, were enlisted by compulsion, and had to put up with hunger and worse; commissars and officers ('commanders') lacked for nothing.

11   Jason Garner, *El Primer Exilio. Los libertarios españoles en Francia antes de la Segunda República*, http://www.academia.edu/11181022/El_primer_exilio._Los_libertarios_espa%C3%B1oles_en_Francia_antes_de_la_Segunda_Republica).

12   In late 1921, Jason Garner, *Goals and Means, Anarchism, Syndicalism, and Internationalism in the Origins of the Federación Anarquista Ibérica*, Edinburgh: AK Press, 2016, p. 192.

13   The Intersyndicale Ouvrière de Langue Espagnole en France.

14   The conference was held between 16-21 December 1920, involving representatives of the CSR, FAUD, FORA, IWW, NAS, SAC, British Shop Stewards, as well as the Russian CP and Profintern. Jason Garner, 'Separated by an "Ideological Chasm": (as above), pp. 307-08. Wilkens was also present at a FAUD conference held on 6 and 7 March 1921.

15   *Bicel (Boletín Interno de la fundación de Estudios Libertarios Anselmo Lorenzo)*, April 2014; http://fal.cnt.es/sites/all/documentos/bicel/BICEL%2022.pdf

Suggestions for Further Reading

Oskar Anweiler: *The Soviets*, New York: Pantheon, 1974.

Autogestion et socialisme, No. 18-19, Paris, 1972.

Jonathan Aves, *Workers Against Lenin*, London: Tauris, 1996.

Paul Avrich, *The Russian Anarchists*, Edinburgh, AK Press, 2006.

Paul Avrich, Ed., *The Anarchists in The Russian Revolution*, London, Thames & Hudson, 1973.

Maurice Brinton, *The Bolsheviks and Workers' Control*, London: Solidarity, 1970.

David Mandel, 'The Factory Committee Movement in the Russian Revolution', in Immanuel Ness & Dario Azzellini, Eds., *Ours to Master and to Own*, Chicago: Haymarket, 2011.

Alexandre Skirda, *Les Anarchistes, les soviets et la révolution de 1917*, Les Éditions de Paris, 2000.

Steve Smith, *Red Petrograd: Revolution in the Factories, 1917-18*, Cambridge University Press, 1983.

Voline, *The Unknown Revolution*, Detroit & Chicago: Black & Red and Solidarity, 1974.

Anthony Zurbrugg, 'Leninism's fault lines: Looking back to 1917', in Leo Panitch and Greg Albo, Eds, *Rethinking Revolution: Socialist Register 2017*, London: Merlin Press, 2016.

Online:
Alternative Libertaire, July-August 2017, Dossier: 1917 http://www.alternativelibertaire.org/?Dossier-1917-Edito-Les-anarchistes-leur-role-leurs-choix

Other Titles from Anarres Editions

BAKUNIN: SELECTED TEXTS 1868-1875
Mikhail Bakunin

Edited and translated by A.W. Zurbrugg

This book brings together a selection of texts: letters, a lecture, newspaper articles, finished and unfinished works. The selection begins in 1868, the year Bakunin moved to Geneva and became a member of the local section of the IWA. Bakunin discusses the development of politics in and around the IWA.

Many of these texts appear here in English for the first time.

'... a book that anyone interested in a viable future for humanity, regardless if s/he identifies or not as anarchist, ought to read.'
Anarkismo

ISBN 978-0-85036-722-5
paperback 300 pages

SOCIAL-DEMOCRACY AND ANARCHISM
in the International Workers' Association, 1864-1877
Rene Berthier

Translated by A.W. Zurbrugg

This book explores the conflicts that took place in the First International. Social and economic conditions varied greatly in Europe in the 1860s and 1870s.

'an excellent work, recommended to both anarchist activists and those interested in the rise of modern revolutionary anarchism.'
Anarchist Studies

ISBN 978-0-85036-719-5
paperback 236 pages

www.merlinpress.co.uk